Sapelo's People

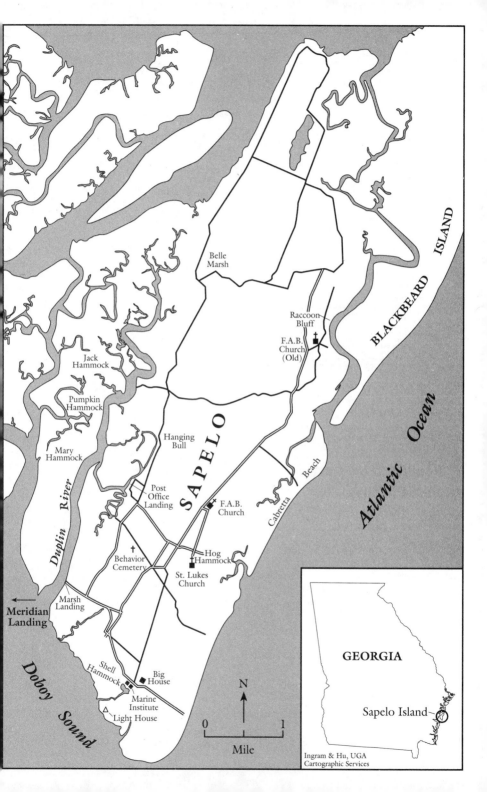

Belle
Marsh

Jack
Hammock

Pumpkin
Hammock

Mary
Hammock

Raccoon
Bluff

F.A.B.
Church
(Old)

BLACKBEARD ISLAND

Atlantic Ocean

SAPELO

Hanging
Bull

Duplin River

Post
Office
Landing

F.A.B.
Church

Cabretta Beach

Behavior
Cemetery

Hog
Hammock

St. Lukes
Church

Marsh
Landing

Meridian
Landing

Shell
Hammock

Big
House

Marine
Institute
Light House

Doboy Sound

N

0   1
Mile

GEORGIA

Sapelo Island

Ingram & Hu, UGA
Cartographic Services

By William S. McFeely

Yankee Stepfather:
General O. O. Howard and the Freedmen

Grant: A Biography

Frederick Douglass

Sapelo's People:
A Long Walk into Freedom

Sapelo's People

A Long Walk into Freedom

William S. McFeely

W · W · Norton & Company

New York　　London

The text of this book is composed
in 10. 5/ 13. 5 Electra
with the display set in
Koch Antiqua Demi- Bold.
Composition by
The Maple- Vail Book Manufacturing Group
Manufacturing by
The Haddon Craftsmen
Book design and illustrations
by Margaret M. Wagner

Library of Congress Cataloging- in- Publication Data
McFeely, William S.
Sapelo's people : a long walk into freedom / William S. McFeely.
p.   cm.
1. Sapelo Island (Ga.) —History. 2. Sapelo Island (Ga.) —
Civilization.   I. Title.
F292. M2M34   1994
975. 8´737—dc20   93- 45968

ISBN 0- 393- 31377- 8

W. W. Norton & Company, Inc.
500 Fifth Avenue, New York, N. Y. 10110

W. W. Norton & Company Ltd.
10 Coptic Street, London WC1A 1PU

1 2 3 4 5 6 7 8 9 0

For

Clara, Laura, and Jackson
and for
Vann

Contents

Sapelo's People

1

Meridian Dock

I went back to the island, went back to a place I scarcely
know and yet feel compelled to come to know, to a scatter-
ing of houses on roads, not all of which I've taken, to Hog
Hammock. The way was by boat, but the community lies
well up in the island's interior, where, walking gingerly, I
am drawn in. I went back to Sapelo Island, Georgia, for
the 125th anniversary of the First African Baptist Church.

Sapelo—the accent is on the first syllable—is one of
the large low-lying barrier islands that stretch along the
South Carolina coast and the 110 miles of the Georgia
coast. From the mainland—the "other side" to the islanders—it is a remote dark stretch on the horizon, barely visible beyond nearer would-be islands—rounded anchored
floating rafts of dense, tall grass—through which a channel of seawater snakes its way to find a habitable island
shore.

Barrier islands, for geologists, are protective armor
shielding a mainland's true coast. Sapelo, for its people, is

a barrier against intrusion; its waterways a passage warily taken to the mainland. On its back side, low dunes stand a feeble guard against the Atlantic Ocean. Harrowing accounts of the drownings when the sea overran Sapelo in 1824 and 1898 demonstrated their vulnerability. The ocean, beautiful, is a troubling power.

There are some ten thousand high-ground acres on Sapelo, better than five thousand more of marsh. The northern two-thirds of the island is wooded, largely with pines. Rows of ancient oaks tell of demarcations where once there were fields to pass, houses and barns to reach, a great beach to explore. Four and a half miles of salt marsh ribboned with tidal creeks north of the main channel separate islanders from the mainland; the Atlantic Ocean lies to the east. None of those ten thousand acres are more than a score or so feet above the sea; on 434 of them, in a partial clearing, sits Hog Hammock.[1] Sapelo's people, sixty-seven of them, live there.

Their forebears lived on the island. On Sapelo and the score of other sea islands, shiploads of thousands of slaves were brought to clear the land and plant, tend, and harvest the rice and fine long-staple cotton that made fortunes for men who owned them. Sapelo's people today are descendants of slaves of Thomas Spalding, who died in 1851. Some he bought along with the land on which they were already owned; many more were bought in the decade after 1802, the year in which Spalding began engorging the island and making it a plantation that ranked among the largest in productive acreage and in number of slaves in Georgia. These people and their children lived and labored on the island as slaves for half a century.

In the first fall of the Civil War—on November 8,

1861—the United States Navy entered the harbor of Port Royal, South Carolina, to blockade Charleston. On the 24th, ships reached Tybee Island, Georgia, to close the way into Savannah and began patrolling the defenseless, exposed islands reaching south to Florida. Many of the island planters left, leaving their slaves behind to fend for themselves. Others, like Thomas Spalding's heirs, ordered their slaves onto boats and, on the mainland, marched them 163 miles into the interior of Georgia, where it was hoped they would be out of way of Union forces. The hope wasn't worth much. The people marched from Sapelo found themselves directly in the path of General Sherman's 1864 March to the Sea.

The islanders I was on my way to visit are descendants of those people, who, slaves no more, walked back to Sapelo. They struggled their way to the coast following Sherman, or on their own. When the war these Southerners had won was over in 1865, Carters and Walkers, Grovners, Hoggs, and Bells came home.

On a Thursday morning a century and a quarter later, turning left from the meandering coastal road at Meridian, I've followed the red-and-white sign out the narrow road to the dock. There was no wait; the *Sapelo Queen* was ready to board. There was just time to look across the marsh grass to the left to see the lacings of nets looped from angled spars high over shrimp boats tied up at the next dock. The wide, oiled planking of the Meridian dock had a familiar feel to me from waiting to go out to Sapelo with groups from my university, and my footing on the gangway was sure as I hauled gear down onto the boat's deck. I knew the ropes, or wanted to feel that I did.

The winter brown of the spartina grass that I remembered from those earlier visits had yielded to a green so lush the clumps looked about to fall into the channel, full at high tide with a rushing chop. The blotched stone of the abandoned lighthouse at Sapelo's south end came closer, as the captain, following the tricky channel, pulled away and then cut back toward Sapelo's Marsh Landing dock. Two dolphins pitched and ducked as we came up to the pilings.

Greg Bailey was there.[2] Dark and fit in his tank top, his turned eye making his quizzical smile the more compelling, he helped cram groceries and bags of clothing and a computer—too heavy, too much—into his sour-green Chevrolet, its top half gone as if into lichen and its defunct ignition system replaced with a toggle switch. Turning away from the roads going off to the south end, he drove up the incongruously dead-straight road through the island's center.

We had skirted the south end of the island, where I had stayed before. The University of Georgia has a marine research facility in the stables of a once luxurious playground of two twentieth-century barons, one a Northerner, the other a Southerner. The first of them, Howard E. Coffin, from Detroit, had acquired his holdings on the island from the last of the land-poor family of slaveholders, who had never again gotten crops and labor together profitably.

On the site of the planter's ruined house, a Sunset Boulevard mansion was built and celebrities were housed, but now the house, on its way to ruin once more, is used by the university for weekend retreats.[3] In its circus room—a playroom decorated as a circus tent—everything from fungi that unexpectedly choose to grow in sand and on

barnacles to the religious practices of the Kiowa is discussed with the irresistibly distracting beauty of the island
beckoning at the windows.

I had been lucky enough to be part of one of the best
of these retreats, but even as we met in seminars whose
topics were germane to the lives of those who live, who
lived, north of the big house, my mind wandered to Hog
Hammock, which we had only glimpsed on field trips.

My curiosity was heightened when I brought students
working with me in a seminar on coastal culture to the
island. Greg's mother, Cornelia Bailey, proud and handsome, the island's chronicler and its most ardent, outspo-
ken champion, met with us to tell of the island's history.
But, as informative as this was, it seemed somehow wrong
that she had to come to the big house, that the women
cooking for us in the mansion's kitchen were the people
of the island whose world we wanted to know. We were
gaining on our knowledge the next day when Cornelia and
her husband, Julius, took us out along a marsh creek to
show us the ways of oystering and fishing. (Effortlessly,
two handfuls of net arched from his hands and fell across
the water in a perfect circle of spiderwebbed line.) I was
beginning to learn, but a distance still barred.

I was curious. I wanted to know the Hog Hammock people in their own world, to meet them in a place that was
not alien to us both. I knew that I wanted to put the south
end behind me. On this visit I was going to stay in Hog
Hammock itself and explore its roads, on which stand,
unevenly, its small, worn, but not quaint houses; walk
down its wood paths, along which the island's dead cars

sink into engulfing brush. (Used cars miraculously appear on Sapelo and miraculously run until they won't, but they don't leave.) I was determined, too, to attend a service in one of the community's two Baptist churches. The younger is St. Luke's, where a visiting preacher leads the service on second Sundays; its elder sister is the First African Baptist Church, which, on its regular first Sunday, would, tomorrow, celebrate being a century and a quarter old.

Greg turned from the macadam onto the sand road, and the first of the oddly scattered houses were to our left and right. Greg's uncle Alfred Bailey's neat single-story house was down a lane to the right. (These Baileys have the island's biggest batch of small children.) Just ahead is a cluster of trailers behind which is Cornelia and Julius— and Greg—Bailey's yellow house.

As we left the road and cut across the cropped grass toward the trailer where I would be staying, Greg, in the laconic way that islanders talk of death and deer tracks, reported that there were people in his mother's other trailer. Two Texans were making a documentary film. Any expectation that I would be the lone visitor in Hog Hammock was gone. But I felt no jealousy of their great clumsy cameras; I was counting on another way into this world. My boarding pass is one issued to historians. My seat on a Hog Hammock porch is a comfortable one because, as we talk, the people I am conversing with come to know that I know something more than hearsay about their world. The past is powerfully with these people, as it is with me. We have it in common.

This spring, in the May warmth of the trailer, comfortable in its fifties furniture but feeling a little shut in, shut out, I take stock. Should anything more be said about an island that has so often piqued Sunday-supplement curiosity? The keeper of the kingdom, Cornelia Bailey, angry and articulate, is not sure. "Take a number and get in line" is her breezy, caustic advice in the face of the storming of Sapelo by curiosity seekers ranging from academic African linguists to real estate predators. Will I be just one more intruder on the island's fierce, frightened privacy?

Bouncing on the springless rears of ancient trucks lurching along roads to the island's beautiful Cabretta beach, I wondered about the houses, the people, but good liberals at the wheel had cautioned that outsiders would not be welcome in Hog Hammock. I had heard, but did not want to heed, this advice. One psychologist who came to do a demographic study twenty years ago became so intimate with some of her "informants" that she has vowed to write about them only when they are dead, and tries to wave other writers off. Her stand at the gate is motivated by her stern regard for the people's privacy and not by territorial jealousy. She senses a fear, not a mere reluctance, among members of the Hog Hammock community that they will be violated, displaced, by exposure, by the telling of their stories.

But is such a lofty remove justifiable in all cases? Must the story be a gaudy invasion of privacy that will jeopardize Hog Hammock's very continuance? I respect others' decisions not to intrude should I make the same one? Isn't the opposite of intrusive exploitation sometimes self-protective reticence? Can't silence be both patronizing and wrong? If averting the eye of the privileged—privileged with education and practice in writing—were to be the only action taken in such situations, wouldn't the story of Sapelo's people and others similarly valuable be lost?

If that advice had been taken, we would not have had

some of the most sensitive renderings that exist of Southern life. To take just two examples, Jack Leigh, a red-
bearded Savannah photographer, in *Nets and Doors*, took
us out to sea with the shrimp fishermen off from the other
Meridian dock, and, flambeaux lighting the way, he followed as the last of the old-time gatherers went out in their
bateaux in *Oystering*. We cannot afford the loss of Leigh's
image of the splendidly dignified Nealy Frippe at the
seemingly undignified work of shucking oysters.

Nor without another outsider's work would we know
about a singular radical sharecropper, Ned Cobb. His
remarkable story, once in danger of being lost, is, as thousands of readers and theatergoers have discovered, safe and
strong in Theodore Rosengarten's *All God's Dangers*. To
tell that story, Rosengarten committed a colossal intrusion, the trapping of a life in a tape recorder. What
resulted was the story of a brave man. Would anyone,
including Frippe and Cobb themselves, view as a violation
the revealing by Leigh and Rosengarten of what they had
learned?

There is no one on this globe who does not want to be
paid attention to, counsels one friend. Perhaps I can pay
honorable attention. Anyway, it's time for a walk.

2

Hog Hammock

Glasco Bailey

Up the sand road, on the right facing a field yielding now to cows and invading trees, is Glasco Bailey's place. (He's Julius's uncle.) His house is an aging, battered, gray-boarded, room-before-room, one-story dwelling fronted by a screened porch. Across a grassless side yard Bailey raises turkeys. They come in all sizes and scurry in cadres, constantly, restlessly stretching and scratching for the grain that he handfuls toward them. There are classic toms that actually do fan their tails and pronounce gobble, gobble, gobble; medium-sized hens scramble along with medium-sized chicks, small hens with small chicks. Hunks of fence, sometimes attached to boards, sometimes not, slant imperfectly more as a statement of defiance to the hawks than as surefire protection from them. In a coop scarcely more than a box, one hen sprawls nesting, ready to bring out the next of endless generations.

Glasco Bailey, bent but agile, presides over his flock of clumsy birds. He raises them not as a product to be eaten, but so they can be—so that they can bring more turkeys into being. They are Glasco Bailey's charges, they and his memories. There is so much of the island that he has known. In that field just across from his place, he once planted rice. Behind his house, only a few hundred yards through dense growth and as out of sight as out of mind, is the great wide, flat beach and the ocean. Never swam in it, he says—sharks; the quieter water of the island's inland side is for swimming.

The shrimp fishermen of the island no doubt knew the sea too well to be romantic about it, but it is hard to know why it seems to have so little attraction for the people of Hog Hammock. Perhaps some of the visitors on anniversary day would commandeer a pickup truck and sneak a look at, or a swim in, that day's calm, warm spring surf, yet, save for an occasional dragging of fish nets carried chest-high at right angle to the water's edge, I doubt if the Atlantic is paid much attention.

Glasco Bailey gives me the look of a patient primary-school teacher as he says yes to the dumbest of the questions I have asked him; of course he will be at the anniversary service tomorrow. And he makes it clear that I will be welcome too, That anniversary has me thinking history. Going back 125 years takes me to 1866, close on the ending of the Civil War, and my curiosity is up. In fact, present darts to past not only on this visit when I will attend a historic holiday, but on all my trips to Hog Hammock. Almost every experience evokes a past not gone by.

This is certainly true as Bailey talks about his brothers, all now dead. What, years back, made one brother—

white-bearded and handsome in a photograph proudly shown to me—move to the then-independent black community on Cumberland Island farther south along the coast, what took another into the army for World War II? He came back and is buried in the island's cemetery. Like many men with no immediate family of their own— Glasco and his wife, Rosa Walker Bailey, who died a dozen years ago, had no children—Bailey finds family immensely interesting. Proudly he brings out the family Bible, in which is inscribed, "Glasco Bailey was borned July 10, 1913." That dating, that Bible, is a cornerstone of the island.

Madeline Hudley Carter

"That was the long-ago time."[1] Mrs. Matty Carter stood in her fastidiously neat shrubbery garden farther along the road and around to the left from Mr. Bailey's. She was looking across to the old dance hall. Starkly beautiful, the sturdy thirty-by-twenty bleached-pine building rises across the overgrown field surrounded by pines younger than the days she remembers. The hall is abandoned now—someone stores food for a cow there—but Matty Carter recalls the life it contained, remembers the dances held in the downstairs. Upstairs was the room where the men's lodge met—the lecterns of the lodge masters are still there.

When she was a girl, the field between her house and the hall was the girls' softball field—no boys allowed. The big game was on the Fourth of July. Matty did not live in Hog Hammock then; she was raised in Shell Hammock on the south end of Sapelo by Mary Olane, the friend of the mother whom she almost never knew. Madeline—Madeline Hudley—was the name her mother, Nancy Roberts Hudley, gave her; she died when Matty was an infant. Matty never knew her father, York Hudley; her mother remains—in memories she was taught by Mary Olane.

As she reached into adolescence, Matty could go off to the dances but only with another, older girl who had guaranteed to get her home and in bed in proper time. She remembers Laura Dixon taking her to one dance; she guesses Laura is the only one of her "bodyguards" still alive—she left the island sixty years ago.

The young people were not allowed into the hall until the older people had had their dance. But then there were the Charleston and waltzes, the two-step and the one-step—not the "breakdown dances the kids do today." The music was from a mouth organ and tubs as drums; later Howard Coffin gave the hall a piano and some standard drums; they're said to still be in the hall, locked in a closet.

"Were you a good dancer?" I ask her.

"I liked the Charleston." Her eyes brighten and for a minute you can see the still trim Matty Carter on the dance floor, a wonderful body alive with the best of the twenties dances.

Loneliness is today's terror. And her candid recollection of what it is to be not lonely comes forth as advice. If you've got a husband or a wife, hang on; it's no fun being alone in bed. Not being alone was worth the battles; the old saying was "Teat and Tom will bite"; a woman and a man have to go after one another. But when she did her going after, Jake, her husband, would just sit there, silent, while she railed. Then, when she paused for breath, he'd ask, "You done had your sermon?" Matty Carter remembers even Jake Carter's silencings with affection.

Jake Carter, one of ten children, was born in 1910 and raised in the house next door.[2] His father, Prince Carter, was "not from here," Mrs. Carter reports, but from Thunderbolt, a community (near Savannah) "on the other side," the standard term for anywhere on the mainland. One formal reccrd, painstakingly researched, suggests that March Carter, of Sapelo, adopted Jake's father and gave the child his brother's name, Prince Carter. Name changes were not uncommon, particularly in the two decades after the Civil War as people on the island reassembled into families altered by the separations of wartime slavery. In any case, Jake grew up firmly anchored on Sapelo.

When Jake Carter came of age and left this mooring, it was as a shrimp fisherman. He worked the boats that fished the waters around the island, but often was off for two and three months on boats that went far down the Florida coast and up into the Gulf of Mexico. The Carters raised six children; three are still living. Matty Carter has seven grandchildren and ten great-grandchildren. One daughter lives on the island, and a granddaughter and her husband come over from Brunswick, the small port city forty miles to the south, to give her a hand with the yard and the woodpile.

When she speaks of the past, Matty Carter longs for things gone. But she does not mourn; her memories are too lively for that. They speak of all that was alive on the island. Unlike her good friend Glasco Bailey—"Co," she calls him—who lives almost in sight of her front porch, she did like going to the ocean. Once you got there on a straight stretch of road that cut cleanly between her place and Bailey's—cut through cedars to the east and the sea. The cedar trees went in a hurricane, the road is just an easy woods trail now, and the cedar-planked boardwalk across the marshes that Matty's son remembers from boyhood is gone; then it was the way to take for walks on the wide flat beach—"black people and white people swam there"—and for Saturday and Sunday evening picnics.

Things used to happen on the island. There was a sawmill at the Long Tabby clearing. Long Tabby itself, once a sugar mill, is built of the coast's famous oyster shell building material, tabby. Its remains have been converted to house the island's post office. Closer still, Charles Hall had a store with groceries and gossip that Matty Carter remembers and misses. Now, "when Uncle Sam sends her paycheck," she calls Bluestein's, the supermarket in Darien, Sapelo's shopping town, on the other side. There on Mondays and Thursdays boxes are filled, cursorily labeled with names so familiar—"M. Cart.," "J. Wils'n"—a glance identifies them, and delivered to the dock. Once on the island, some neighbor—perhaps Caesar Banks, who also sees to it that the wall behind her wood-burning stove is safely backed with tabby—without any need for instruction, drops the box off at her house. Stocking up once a month, the woman who once cooked for sophisticated guests in the island's big house is not treating herself as grandly as she did them.

Stories of life in that big house provoke a double cloud of wistfulness and resentment. There was a dependence on those white households in which women like Matty worked as domestic servants. "If only she had lived, I

wouldn't have had anything to worry about": Matty Carter
is talking of the next-to-last of the mistresses of the house,
who took her with her to Palm Beach when she moved
from Sapelo. But when Matty got there, although she
stayed in touch with that possible benefactor, she knew
she had to turn right around and come back to Hog
Hammock.

I tell her it's not the big house or the big white families,
but Hog Hammock that I need to know about. She agrees.
This is where the life is, the light; the other was a shadow.
Many would say the other was the real world, but here in
her yard the structures of rich people's lives seem alien
to reality.

Allen Green

Just to the west of Matty Carter's place, across Sapelo's
main north-south sand road, is a faded red-on-white sign:

> The Basket-Maker
> Allen Green
> Sapelo Island, Ga.

Green's baskets are works of art—an art derived in
method and pattern from Africa—and visitors interested
in the coastal culture seek him out. I've met Green before,
but now I'm not with a group; on one visit the two of us
sit on a wooden bench in his front yard. Narrow slivers of
palmetto fronds are softening in a galvanized tub; Allen
Green sits in a nest of sweet grass that swirls as well around
our feet. His small penknife peels the palmetto; with its

point he presses the circling, spiraling strip between the circling rows, never stopping his stories.

Green's recollections are rich and reach beyond his own long past back to grandfather and namesake, Allen Smith. A "monkey who could fit any wrench" is the way the grandson admiringly recalls his small, able grandfather. "Smart fellow," Allen Smith was the blacksmith who could shoe horses, the woodworker who could make shingles, the mechanic who could fix any farm machinery, and—luckily for his grandson—a master basketmaker.

"Named for my grandfather. Came from Macon . . . when peace came." It was he who, more than seventy years ago, taught his grandson how to make the basket sitting now in Allen Green's lap. Rapidly, coil on coil, a saucered fourteen-inch circle of tightly woven tan-and-green sweetgrass has grown from his constantly flexing hands. Too clever for my own good, I am amused by the irony that Allen Green learned an African art from someone who lived far inland rather than from a forebear on the sea island coast where romantics so determinedly look to find, and so find, Africa washed ashore. (A lot later, I learn that Allen Smith did not come from Macon, he came back from Macon.)

Like many, perhaps most, of the residents of Hog Hammock, Allen Green moved there fairly recently, in the 1950s. Since then, Sapelo's people have lived in one hammock. Once there was Belle Marsh over on the west side of the island, almost as far north as Chocolate, a farm site high on a bluff above the Mud River where a splendid barn still stands; Hanging Bull was inland, while Moses' Hammock was at the head of the Duplin River, which partly separates Sapelo from Little Sapelo Island, on which were Mary, Pumpkin, and Jack's Hammocks; at the far south end of Sapelo was Shell Hammock, and five miles north of Hog Hammock was Raccoon Bluff.

That bluff twenty feet above the clear Mud River is at the northeast shoulder of the island. Standing on the grassy knoll of the bluff you look across the widening water to heavily wooded Blackbeard Island, which slips down in front to the topmost thrust of Sapelo; to your right, the river reaches for and meets the ocean, which sprawls beyond a south-reaching sandbar in a glare of pale light. At your back are old trees, with a thicket of new growth crowding in behind. Nowhere is there any sign of habitation, any indication of human activity, save, perhaps, a shrimp boat far off at the horizon.

Reluctantly, the residents of Raccoon Bluff, the last of whom was Allen Green, swapped their homes there for houses, all of a kind, with electricity and plumbing, and smaller plots of land, in Hog Hammock. Richard J. Reynolds, Jr., the heir to a tobacco fortune and owner after Coffin of all of the island that these people didn't own, was creating a hunting and wildlife preserve of the whole north end of the island. Green swore he would never move; he yielded when Reynolds threatened to close the road to the bluff. "Allen Green wouldn't move till hell freezed over," reports Matty Carter. "Well, hell ain't freezed over and Allen Green right here."

So Allen Green lives now in Hog Hammock, but his memories are rich and strong of Raccoon Bluff. Stories pour from him as we go there in his old blue pickup, which has gear trouble. Detouring on a boggy rutted wood road to get past a truck parked smack in the middle of the straight one-lane road running to the north of the island, we turn right toward the bluff, brush scraping the sides of the pickup. Soon Allen Green is pointing out clearings, closing in, where he was raised and both his grandfathers were raised, where his wife's family's place was, where an aunt lived. All the houses were pulled down; only his memory can locate them now.

Standing on the bluff, he points well out into the river to where one grandfather's house once stood. Man and nature have both been at work depleting his island; erosion has cut back the bluff one hundred yards. As a boy—he left the island at fourteen—he swam across to Blackbeard Island another hundred yards away; there was a swarm of kids who did—"ten, fifteen." It would have been a young boy's paradise. And not bad for the boy's parents and grandparents either, although for an immensely energetic boy there did not seem to be much ahead of him save the scraping by of farming. His father and grandfather, James Green, Jr. and Sr., and the close-by Walkers—when his first wife died, Allen married Annie Mae Walker, whom he had grown up with—farmed their own land. One still-clear field of wild grass was their rice field. There were oxen to pull a plow or a wagon and horses, too, to get you to the other hammocks. Or you walked.

Allen Green knows his family back farther than I know mine—I cannot name my great-grandparents with certainty, he can. But beyond that point we are both in debt to those who, from records, not recollection, have retrieved Sapelo's past. Ten years ago, a professional gene-alogist, hired by Georgia's Department of Natural Resources as part of an effort to untangle the record of landownership, partly subverted that purpose by compiling astonishingly full records of forty-four Sapelo families. We now know their stories with a richness of detail that far outvalues the simple data assembled on their assets. Mae Ruth Green (no relation to Allen Green save in the friendship they achieved as she worked) has documented a past once blurred in sentimental lore.

The island has, in fact, defied ownership. It has not always been the Hog Hammock people's island, nor did possession hold for the Southern planters or their twentieth-century successors. It hasn't long or clearly been the state's. For at least two thousand years before Europeans— Spanish, English, and even French—lived there, it was lived on by changing groups of Indians—there is an ancient shell ring on the island's west side. Africans were brought to Sapelo as well, how early isn't clear. What we do know with assurance is that Sapelo has been home to the Baileys, the Carters, the Greens for just short of two hundred years. Everyone has long known, vaguely, that these people are the descendants of people brought to Sapelo as slaves early in the nineteenth century. But, thanks to Mae Ruth Green's careful interviews, substantiated and greatly added to by her archival research, we now know far more than that an anonymous group of slaves labored on the island. We know these people—we know their names—we know the forebears of everyone alive now in Hog Hammock.

And so, when I talk to Glasco Bailey, to Matty Carter, to Allen Green, I can reach back past remembered grandparents and great-grandparents to the first members of these families to be brought to Sapelo. And soon I am back to Bilali, not the "legendary Muslim slavedriver" of so many vague reminiscences, but Allen Green's great-great-great-grandfather.

3

Behavior

I go looking for Bilali in Behavior, the island's cemetery. The graveyard is as irregularly plotted as were the hammocks once scattered over the island; as oddly angled as the stance of the houses in Hog Hammock today. And the uneasy grass is less level than the road under oaks and pines that takes you to the graveyard, which, incongruously, is not out of earshot or even sight of the south end's airstrip, where a small plane infrequently stumbles into the air.

There are many, too many, fresh heaps of sand stuck round with yard-high buckets of imitation flowers complete with the funeral parlor's plastic-wrapped index cards identifying the deceased. (On one grave, real gladioluses wither.) Gravestones stand at ornery angles, only roughly grouped in families. None is large, none ornate. (I'm told some ornaments have been stolen, those said to be African in form.) The legends are simple, "Peace at Last" or "At Rest"; there are few symbols, no crosses or vases as vessels of life. What is on the stones are names and dates, often scratched inexpertly—poignantly—by a hand resolved that cost will not determine whether a remembrance is assured.

Behavior is an odd name for a cemetery, but it makes sense on Sapelo Island, where people have a good enough sense of humor to be at home in a community called Hog Hammock. And a visitor to the island doesn't find it strange, either. No, Behavior, its grounds uneven and grass-choked, its stones akimbo—the way things are in this world—suggests life rather than death.

The sadness that inhabits all cemeteries is present in Behavior, of course. But not even the inevitable reminders of mortality justify predicting an end of the community. Those who shake their heads over the undeniable fact that few young people stay on the island, that many of the sixty-seven residents of Hog Hammock are old, don't have it quite right. Such doomsayers may see only a morbid finality in a book written with one eye on a graveyard. But "behavior" is the word for the actions of people; there is a nice ironic liveliness in its use as the name of a cemetery.

Wandering by, I sense grief here. But somehow there is also abundant evidence in the names and dates on the gravestones of the connectedness of people, of the continuity of life. The stones are not mile markers lugubriously beckoning to those with these same names living in nearby Hog Hammock. It works the other way; the stones speak with eagerness of the past of people with both feet still firmly in this world. They wake me to the stretch backward of life. The names and ages and dates stubbornly, insistently demand attention.

Walking among the gravestones, among the families, I

cannot find Bilali. All of the death dates are from the time of freedom, after he died. I cannot find his name, but I do come across one stone that reads:

MINTO BELL
DIED AUG 25 1890
AGE 110 YRS
SWEET BE HER REST

Minto Bell was Bilali's daughter; Bilali was the island's patriarch and during his long lifetime a legend. But he was not legendary. There are vivid documented accounts of a man who fascinated every visitor to Sapelo, and Bilali himself gave us one of the truly firm grasps we have on him. About 1855, near the end of his very long life, Bilali gave away a handsome leather-bound book of fine unlined paper with a manuscript text which has perplexed would-be translators ever since.[1] It was written here in America when Bilali was in middle or old age. An analysis of the penetration of the ink's iron fibers into the paper on which he wrote establishes the writing's date as 1824, with a lee-way of fifteen years on either side.[2] The ink is blotched, the penmanship and particularly the spelling are tortured. One scholar has conjectured that it was the work of a one-time scholar of the law, as there is a possible reference to a well-known legal treatise.[3] But closer examination makes it clear that Bilali's message is religious; half-mis-spelled, there is on the first page the intonement "In the name of God the merciful the compassionate may the prayers of God be on our Lord Muhammad and his family and his companions."

Bilali is believed to have been born about 1760 in

Timbo, the capital of Futa Jallon, in the beautiful interior hill country of what is now Guinea. His name, his knowledge of Arabic, and, above all, his prayer make it virtually certain that Bilali was raised a Muslim, and his literacy suggests that he had had some scholarly training in Timbo, which was a center of learning. It is likely that Bilali was a student when he was seized and sold into slavery.

In Futa Jallon, Bilali had the great misfortune of being at a nasty conjunction of the virulent North Atlantic slave trade. North American planters were eager to buy slaves. This was particularly true in Georgia, where "overt" slaveholding was prohibited prior to 1749 and where planters were trying to catch up economically with their fellows in the older plantation colonies, Maryland, Virginia, and the Carolinas, and on the islands of the West Indies.[4]

The second half of the eighteenth century was the time of the greatest number of imports of African slaves into North America.[5] At the same time, Futa Jallon was in the midst of one of a series of eighteenth-century holy wars between rival Muslim factions. As one authority put it, it was difficult to discern whether "the demand for slaves caused the wars of the jihads, rather than the jihads creating a supply of prisoners for sale."[6] In either case, Bilali was sold to slave traders on the coast and exported to the Bahamas, where he fathered the "foreign born" daughters whom Thomas Spalding bought, along with Bilali, and brought to Sapelo.

Once there, Bilali held devoutly to his Muslim faith. His book, his memory, is of his practice of that faith. Explicitly, he gives the directions for washing before prayer: "And his right hand wipes off the [foot] up to the ankle / And his left hand wipes off [the foot] up to the ankle / And he puts both hands / In the water container / And with them wipes his head."[7]

Bilali, known in 1844 to an ethnographer as an "extremely old" man who could "write Arabic," somehow got hold of a blank book—he was already so interesting to visitors that one might well have given him such a book.[8] In it, Bilali gathered up his memory of days of formal learning—memory which could be retrieved only in fragments.[9] Technically, he has misspelled the words, but Ahmad Dallal, a scholar of Arabic and of Islam who has worked over the document with a sensitive eye, conjectures that Bilali recalled with perfect accuracy phrases that had had for him a lifelong importance. Then, saying aloud what he was determined to record, the old man wrote, in his own accent, what he heard himself say: "Possession of all things to Him, all praise to Him. He gives life, he brings death. He has power over all things."[10]

The book is an icon, in the true sense—a holy object connecting Africa to America in the hand of a deeply religious man. Bilali—his name is rendered in a score of ways, Belali, Bel-al-i, Billally (slipping, when given to his grandchildren, into Billy)—reportedly had a great many children. One source mentions twenty-three; we have careful records of four of them and of their descendants.

It is not clear exactly when Bilali was brought to Sapelo, but it must have been close to the year 1802. Thomas Spalding, the man who bought him, and, luckily, also bought at least some of his children, was developing what was to become one of the largest cotton plantations in the Southeast. And one of the most prosperous, thanks to his good fortune in having been in the Bahamas and having encountered Bilali.

Spalding, born in 1774 (and younger than Bilali), was the son of a coastal planter who was a loyalist during the Revolutionary War. The father's extensive holdings in McIntosh and Glynn counties were confiscated, and the family fled to British Florida. When in 1783 Florida was ceded to Spain, the Spaldings moved to the Bahamas.[11]

In 1795, Thomas, back in Georgia, married Sarah Leake, the daughter and heir of the owner of much of Sapelo. On his father-in-law's death in 1802, Spalding and his wife returned from a trip to England; with an inheritance from his own father (who had swiftly restored his fortune), Thomas set about buying laborers with which to embark on a major agricultural enterprise on the island.

Thomas Spalding educated himself as an agricultural scientist and wrote extensively about the raising of a variety of crops. While cotton provided the core of his considerable wealth, he also made money lumbering and raising rice and sugar. And early on (to no avail) he urged his fellow Southern planters not to become dependent on a single crop and experimented with many others.

Cotton, a scraggly plant, was, of course, imperious. The industrial demand for its fibers was insatiable, the profits possible from their production enormous, the labor needed to produce the crop slave. And, ironically, an African slave (along with a Connecticut Yankee) was required to be a pioneer in an agricultural revolution that resulted in the terrible resilience of American slavery. The mechanization of the textile industry created the demand for the stuff, the creation of a machine that could clean the fibers of seed and other particles provided its supply. Eli Whitney's cotton gin made the raising of short-staple cotton profitable across a vast swath of the mainland South.

Such mass production did not, however, preclude huge

fortunes being made growing cotton of higher quality, the famous Sea Island cotton. Thomas Spalding learned to value long-staple black seed cotton while living in the Bahamas, and there is every reason to believe that he bought Bilali precisely because the African knew how to cultivate the superior plant. He brought the slave to Sapelo, and there the two men became among the earliest large-scale cultivators of the finest grade of cotton raised in the United States.[12] Despite the fact that it was not until 1840 that a dependable gin was designed that could clean the delicate island cotton mechanically, it proved to be a highly profitable variety of that commodity—cotton—which was to lock into place America's slave economy.[13]

One of Spalding's descendants reported that he bought "many" slaves in the Charleston market "at one hundred dollars each, or less (with privilege of choice)" and "From the West Indies he brought hands trained for the management and guidance of raw labor."[14] Bilali became a driver on Spalding's plantation, and virtually its manager—and he knew long-staple cotton. That the slave was able to persuade his purchaser to also buy at least some of his children is attested to by one of Bilali's descendants: "He come obuh wid all he daughtuhs grown. He whole family wuz mos grown up."[15]

Spalding was shrewd enough to strike a bargain with a slave he was determined to buy—the purchase of members of his family—that would ensure the slave's cooperation. Once on Sapelo, Bilali was put in charge and required to make the other slaves work according to his expert direction. He brought with him not only his managerial and agricultural skills, but also a commanding personality. Out of his past as a privileged scholar and buttressed by

study than the Gullah language, which developed and survived on the barrier islands of South Carolina and Georgia
because of the relatively low mobility of the slaves who
had been brought there.[22]

The growers of long-staple cotton, coveting slaves who
knew how to raise the crop, managed to get slaves from
single or related language groups in Africa, people who
could talk to each other. With this as a base, they created,
here in America, the creole language Gullah. There are
subtle differences between the speech on one island and
another, but it is the constancy that is striking. The
islands, each remote from its neighbors, would seem to
have afforded little opportunity for conversation among
slaves. But words traveled on a verbal underground railroad as slaves delivered timber from one island to another,
as they met in mainland markets to which they brought
crops.

Bilali's great-granddaughter Katie Brown recalled close
to a century after his death that his daughter—her grandmother—had not yet shed her African dress or ways of
speech. "She ain tie uh head up lak I does," reported Katie
(who wore a head rag) of her grandmother: "she weah a
loose wite clawt da she trow obuh uh head lak veil an it
hang loose on uh shoulduh,"[23] and "she (Magret) speak
funny wuds we didn know. She say 'mosojo' and sometimes 'sojo' wen she mean pot. Fuh watuh she say 'deloe'
an fuh fyuh she say 'diffy.' [Here Katie was correct as to
the function of "deloe" rather than its meaning; "deloe" is
the vessel.] She tell us, 'Tak sojo off diffy.' " That pot
wasn't over the fire when she made a "funny flat cake she
call 'saraka.' . . . I membuh how she make it. She wash
rice, an po off all duh watuh. She let wet rice sit all night,

and in mawnin rice is all swell. She tak dat rice an put it in wooden mawtuh, an beat it tuh paste with wooden pestle. She add honey, sometime shuguh, and make it in flat cake wid uh hans. 'Saraka' she call um."[24]

Magret—Margaret Hillery when she married—made these cakes "same day ebry yeah, an it big day."[25] These were holiday cakes; a holy day was being observed. We know, too, that rice, if it was also a cash crop, was the slaves' food. And well into the twentieth century it was the staple of the island diet—if fish hadn't been caught that day, rice often was all there was to eat. The coarse-grassed meadow where Glasco Bailey wages a constant battle with the pine seedlings that invade, across the road from his house, was, not so long ago, his rice field. Rice for the master's profit was the rice grown in water in elaborately irrigated diced fields; the Hog Hammock rice, not freed by water of weeds, was grown on dry land.

Thomas Spalding extracted a fierce amount of labor from the slaves—probably well over five hundred by 1835—who cleared the island for his cotton and rice crops. (Once his lands were cleared, Spalding, well read in agricultural science, experimented with a diversity of crops, most, like indigo, labor-intensive, some, like olive and mulberry trees, less so.)[26] Hundreds of live oaks were sawn down, trimmed, squared, and hauled by oxen to boats and sold as timber. Other trees were ringed of their bark and, when dead, felled and burned. Stumps were pulled and the woodland floor laboriously cleared of saplings, ditches were dug and salt marshes drained, to create cotton fields. Once the spring planting was up, the soil between the rows of low, bristly bushes was chopped with long-handled hoes to banish weeds and to loosen the soil baking under the intense summer sun. When it came time for harvesting, the cotton was picked into long gunny sacks dragged by stooping workers though the fields that spread over Spalding's four thousand acres.

There is no way to romanticize the back-bending labor these workers were forced to perform. Among the many recorded reminiscences of Bilali and his neighbors, nothing tells us just what these people who were doing the island's labor thought about their work and all of the other aspects of their lives. We do know who those people were, and we have glimpses of them eating and praying. Thanks to Katie Brown, we know with considerable precision how her great-grandparents, Bilali and Phoebe, prayed—to Allah. That faith was not lost, but rather was transferred to another still firmly held. Just after the family was no longer slave, two of Bilali's grandsons were founders of the First Baptist Church. Two faiths, two continents, came together. And Bilali gave us his book—his mystery.

4

"A Wild African Tribe"

No one talks about slavery today on Sapelo. But it is the dead past that is not dead. It slumbers silently on the island as it does all over the South. Only the worst of the haters of the slaves' descendants would want it awakened, and the long decades of overcoming have not prevented slavery's shadow from spreading darkness.

Here on Sapelo there was slavery of the classic North American sort. Over vast stretches of the island, woodlands were cleared and marshes drained by slaves laboring on the Spalding plantation. Money crops—rice, sugar, and cotton—were planted, cared for, and harvested. There is almost no one in Hog Hammock today who is not a descendant of these very slaves. The slave past is, however, too many generations back for there to be much more than the uneven recollection of a great-grandmother's stories when someone does talk about the "slavery days."

This island is unlike other places in the South where,

fortunately, the records of slavery have been preserved. Of Sapelo there are few documents that yield a picture of the lives of the people who lived and worked here. We know from Thomas Spalding's own writings, those of his grandson, and accounts of visitors what work was done here; we do not know precisely which people did what, nor, more important, what they thought about as they labored.

What we do have is another, singular, hold on these people. We know their names. I had the good fortune of talking with Glasco Bailey, Matty Carter, and Allen Green right there in Hog Hammock, of meeting Bankses, Grovners, Walkers, Wilsons, and Johnsons. And, thanks to the astonishing genealogical work of Mae Ruth Green, I can know them in another way; doing assiduous research, she traced the lineage of these families—and more—to forebears who were slaves.

When names emerge, slavery ceases to be an institution, a labor system, an evil, a way of life—an abstraction—and becomes, instead, a populated time. Sapelo is an island whose people have names. We know Carolina Underwood and his wife, Hannah; we know not only that they were born in Africa, but that "deh bote Ibos," an agricultural people who lived just above the delta of the Niger River in what is now Nigeria.[1] That they were from the same (large) region might suggest that they had been together when enslaved and stayed together through all the transactions that ended with their being brought to Sapelo. It is far more likely that like other lonely people seeking some hold on a terrifying world, they discovered they shared a language.

Hannah Underwood knew, with considerable precision, where in Africa she was from and how she was taken.

As her granddaughter Julia Grovner reported: "Muh gran, she Hannah. . . . she tell us how she brung yuh. . . . she wid huh ahnt who wuz diggin peanuts[2] in duh fiel, wid uh baby stop on uh [the aunt's] back. Out uh duh brush two wite mens come. . . . Dey led um in tuh duh woods, weah deah wuz udduh chillun dey done ketched an tie up in saks. Duh baby an Hannah wuz tie up in sacks lik duh udduhs an Hannah nebuh saw huh ahnt agen an nebuh saw de baby agen. Wen she wuz let ou uh duh sack, she wuz on boat an nebuh saw Africa agen."[3]

Brought through the steps of the slave trade, Hannah found herself in the pens of the Charleston slave market where Thomas Spalding bought many of his Sapelo slaves. She never yielded her Ibo identity. Whatever her work, the Spaldings were not permitted to forget the origin of the woman who was doing it. In a reminiscence forty years after Hannah and her husband died, a relative of the Spaldings referred to—identified—her as the "old 'Yebo' nurse, Maam Hannah."[4] The Underwoods shared each other's lives into extreme old age. They died—together—in 1871. Their house caught fire and they were too infirm to move; one of Thomas Spalding's grandsons (whose father Hannah probably had nursed) carried them out, but they died of their burns.

Twentieth-century grandchildren of the Underwoods had, in these family stories, ties to a long African past, and Sapelo grandchildren had a long American past as well. To sit on Hicks Walker's porch and watch his large, sure hands tie the delicate knots of a beautiful throwing net for island fishing is to visit with the son of Gib Walker, a

"longshoreman" (according to the 1910 census) and himself the son of Alexander Walker, a farmer. Alexander,
having reached voting age, registered to vote in 1877, as
did his father, Charles Walker, who had been going to the
polls since 1867—after having lived as a slave for sixty
years. A lot of history sits with you on Sapelo.

It is hard to reach back beyond Sapelo memories to
Africa, or even to the Bahamas, although a legend of a
ship coming from the islands is still alive. There are now
only the shards of recollections of Bilali and Carolina and
Hannah Underwood. As for other descendants of immi-
grants whose coming was so long ago, it is hard to give
some ancient, distant home meaning. Among a few of
the younger members of the community there has been a
conscious effort to achieve that meaning.

With the simultaneous rise of the independent black
African states and the civil rights movement, there was
a powerful drive here in America to establish an African
identity, to construct a connection to an African past.
Like other Americans who have found an ethnic linkage
forced, some travelers to Africa found that pillar of the past
to be hollow. What they observed might be intellectually
compelling, but they had to admit (usually to themselves)
that they were observing as strangers.

And yet, in a basic way, the connection does matter.
Frederick Douglass knew he stuck out like a sore thumb
on most of the prosperous white streets of America (and
rather enjoyed the fact), but, somewhat to his surprise, he
found it reassuring to see on the clamorous, busy docks of
Cairo that most of the people of an admixture of races
looked more or less the way he had when he worked on
Baltimore and New Bedford docks as a young man. He

was, even as he watched from an upper deck, part of a crowd and not apart from it. So too, Cornelia Bailey tells of arriving in Sierra Leone a decade ago and "being at home."

On the other hand, when a scholarly linguist comes to Hog Hammock from Sierra Leone, as Salikoko Mufwene recently did, he can't count too heavily on being of the family. In appearance, he may, at first glance, seem a candidate for kinship. But when, in crisp precision, the linguistic queries are put forward, he finds to his amusement—and frustration—that he's just one more of the seemingly endless procession of curious visiting anthropologists—professional and amateur—asking damn fool questions.

Cornelia Bailey, not only with her trip to Africa but also with her willingness to suffer any fool as long as she can champion Hog Hammock, is an exception to her neighbors. They are not as assertive; even if there were means it seems unlikely that there would be curiosity sufficient to make most of the island's people pack a bag for Africa.

For Cornelia's neighbors the remembered memories, the stories, are all on the Hog Hammock side of the ever-ominous Atlantic Ocean. It is not for crossing or even troubling with save when it rises in a storm. Oceans are for romantics. Sardine-packed sunbathers and solitary walkers crave its edges, are drawn to it, into it. Men who must go to sea to fish or to wrench vessels from one coast of an ocean to another are required to confront and try to master its power, to hold its surface. Some of them secretly know the romance; adventurers who choose the encounters surely do.

Sapelo's people know their ocean differently. On one hand, it is simply there—to be ignored; on the other, it echoes a remote, real past. Africa is on its other side. Sapelo forebears were survivors of the terrible voyages from Africa to America, the Middle Passage, of the dragging from a home and of the cramming into the holds of slavers to endure the torture of an ocean crossing. Their fellow slaves-to-be who did not endure were, dead or dying, thrown into the sea. The ships took those who lived into New World ports. Many who eventually were sold to sea island planters were taken first to the Bahamas, sold, and driven to work. Then, to be sold again, were shipped to Charleston. There as well as in the Bahamas earlier, Thomas Spalding or his agent bought Sapelo's people, who were walked and ferried onto the island. Spalding made them clear his forest, work his fields; they in turn—and not out of choice—made his island their home. Their bitter adopted home.

But their birthplace won't allow itself to be forgotten. There was for Cornelia a reaching for roots, but danger lurks in such memories. Reinventing the original African leave-taking and the American arrival—as well as the voyage between—is an exercise in pain. Something of the terror of the Middle Passage emerges in the prose of a white man who knew the island as a boy and wrote of it eighty years later. Charles Spalding Wylly tells—without names—of the experiences of the first American generation of his grandfather's slaves. Wylly recounts the visit to the island of "Captain Swarbreck, retired, master and owner of the good ship 'Ann.' " He "had spent near fifty of his sixty years in 'trading and voyaging' from the west coast of Africa to Brazil, Cuba and the West Indies.[5]

"Very various in kind and character had been the cargoes carried—palm oil, rare woods, mahogany, ebony, with a little 'dust' from where Bishop Heber tells us, 'Africa's sunny fountains roll down their golden sands,' had of late been most common. In earlier days and past years, cargo after cargo had been listed as 'live stock' and great profits had been credited to the captain's books upon their safe arrival in Havana, Charleston, or Rio. His true nature had been a most kindly one and he hated the whole business, but 'trade is trade,' and if the ship 'Ann' were out of it the barque 'Polly' would be in it. So when forcing the 'Ann' with heavy press of sail with *stock* that moaned, even died, from overcrowding, the captain said to himself: 'The more I load and the quicker I sail, the sooner it will be over and I can quit and lay up in a snug harbor with money enough to live on, and leave to those who bought of me the awaiting of the 'scourge one day or another' to return to their children or their children's children."[6]

The snug harbor found by Swarbreck and his wife was Burbon, a place on the northwestern side of Sapelo once owned by a Frenchman and not much later sold to the Spaldings. That family, profiting from the stock "bought of me," knew not yet of any scourge, and the Spaldings expressed their distaste for the former master of a slaver and his wife only with ostracism. As Wylly told it, "The social position, the education, the birth and tastes of the [Swarbrecks] made it impossible that there should be much intercourse."[7]

Wylly's perspective, not surprisingly, remained focused on his family as he wrote: "I think it may gratify curiosity to tell in what manner these men and women fresh from Africa would with any safety be taken into the life of a family where in all probability there were not three white men to three hundred of their own race."[8] As Wylly begins his account of the arrival of the Sapelo people, he proves that the Spalding place was a classic plantation not in terms of its large size and its cotton crop, but in the fact that, like all other Southern plantations, it was not precisely like any other.

As they brought African slaves onto the remote island, the Spaldings did so according to a plan. They sought safety in the face of great outnumbering. But if there was fear in the big house, a description of that plan hints as well at the terror of those enslaved in Africa, forced into the stinking holds of slave ships, like Swarbreck's, for the Middle Passage, and then driven from those ships and into the slave pens of the Charleston market. Already separated from family and other familiar people, having seen their fellow cargo, dead and no longer of value, thrown into the sea, these were the survivors. Unable to communicate with most of the other people in the pens and shouted at in a language wholly alien, they can scarcely have imagined what would be their fate.

If that fate was to be bought for Sapelo, they would have been herded onto a packet with about forty other people: "slaves were seldom bought at one time in a larger number than fifty, the sexes being generally equal." The purchase, Wylly recalled, "would probably be ten men, ten women, fifteen boys from twelve to fifteen years of age, and the same of girls." Spalding's credit was good; he paid one hundred dollars, and up, for these people—half in cash, half twelve months later, if, leanly fed, they proved to be as healthy as represented. "They were a perishable commodity and were subject to glut."[9]

The "merchandise," carefully chosen in the Charleston market, was ferried to Sapelo and driven onto the landing. There someone had to be able to talk to each of these miserable newcomers, sullen or shaking. Neophytes were matched with those already "seasoned": "Here always would be found a number of men and women acquired in former years who belonged to the same race, frequently of the same tribe and speaking the same dialect, or at least capable of making themselves understood."[10] Slaves already on Sapelo most probably were lined up at the island's dock and, as they found their voices responded to, given the task of sorting the new people. Then, according to Thomas Spalding's careful scheme for establishing units of slaves of a size appropriate to observation and discipline, one man, "chosen for his ability to command and fluency in speech, would be given the ten men, with the right of issuing food when and where he pleased, or to retain it and not call for the daily ration."[11] Not too subtly, a hierarchical structure based on the power of food, of life, was established among the slaves; more subtly, the manipulation of established people into imposing the discipline of masters was achieved, along with the indoctrination of the newcomers.

"To a woman with the same gifts the ten women would be assigned, and to a third [person] the boys and girls," wrote Wylly. Then he added, with considerable ambiguity, "Frequently they were divided between two of different sexes, this being governed by the ages." What was the chronicler driving at—or past? Were the younger children given to a woman and the older to a man? We are told later that instruction in manual labor came only months later, so why the division? It is not possible to tell, but,

Wylly reports, "the birth rate" of the Sapelo slaves "was phenomenal," and he asserts that the chief reason was "the youth and the equality in the number of the sexes."[12] In all purchases not only healthy workers but prospective childbearing appears to have been in the buyer's eye. Hannah Underwood is reported to have borne twenty-two children.

Wylly, adopting the familiar metaphor of slavery as a school, asserted that the "education thus started progressed rapidly." The pupils were segregated, men from women and both from children, and taught plantation discipline. "The reward was good food, . . . bread or its substitutes, such as rice and hominy, . . . was issued daily at the barns on the call only of the preceptor. He lived with them, talked and walked with them. . . . Fish, crabs and such stuff they caught for themselves under the eye and teaching of their constant guide [who was released from other labor] and watchful guard.

"After a tutelage of perhaps three to five months they were assigned to work requiring not skill but manual strength, such as gathering shell for the burning of lime, the mixing of sand, lime and shell into concrete [the famous tabby]—in the mortar beds—still under the eyes of their teacher—and transferring in hand-barrows of the concrete to the moulds which were slowly growing into the walls of house, stable or barn.

"In twelve months they were generally . . . 'tamed,' and had acquired enough of the English language to be understood and to understand when spoken to. Then, and not until then, did their master begin to notice their personal qualities and abilities and assign them to duties which they were best fitted for."[13] The Spaldings had created the fiction that these people had no past, that their lives began in the school of slavery which brought them from unintelligibility to the possession of personality and of an understanding sufficient to undertaking of specific tasks.

The carefully orchestrated indoctrination plan did not always work. A much-garbled legend told to explain "Behavior" as a place-name has "a considerable number of negroes belonging to a wild African tribe" rebelling against the mentors to which they were assigned. They bolted and "betook themselves to the woods." As the story goes, "Mr. Spalding permitted them to remain unmolested for three weeks and then took an interpreter and went to see them, making promises of beef and other food if they would come to the plantation and join other slaves."[14] These negotiations, in which Spalding apparently depended on coaxing (and perhaps threats and warnings of starvation) rather than outright force, were designed to alter the "behavior" of these "wild" Africans and bring them within the plantation's civil order.

It is difficult to reconstruct just how the Spalding plan of indoctrination, of behavioral control, played out. His grandson, not surprisingly, insists that "no cruelty of any kind was practiced or relied upon." He even contended that "in this early stage of plantation life on the seacoast was to be found the happiest form of peasant life that the country could offer."[15] The period he was referring to was the nineteenth century's first decade, when the importation of slaves was still legal and when Thomas Spalding was purchasing these people. For Charles Wylly this was the "early and almost initiative stage . . . in the evolution of the rudest and most primal form of men into a higher state of civilization before there had been born into him a love of personal rights, not physical freedom." (For Wylly, slavery, *"in its first stage,"* was not "an unmitigated evil. It is an apprenticeship through which a race becomes worthy of freedom. The wrong is in its continuation after the man or race has become worthy of freedom.")[16]

The desperate attempt of the Behavior slaves to establish a maroon—a secret place of refuge for slaves (or others) escaping authority—right on the island makes clear that all was not as tranquil as Wylly contends. An island, of course, has its moat, but a swimmer with any proficiency at all could swim to the uninhabited Blackbeard Island to Sapelo's north. Still, even the most defiant slave might have hesitated with warnings of no fresh water, plenty of poisonous snakes, and no food other than the immensely prolific oysters and mussels.

The newly arrived "wild" slaves were not the only ones who wanted out; in 1807 Thomas Spalding offered a twenty-dollar reward for the return of Landau, a slave bought from one of the Frenchmen who had lived on Sapelo. The runaway was "a Negro Man . . . about five feet nine inches high, stout and well made, pleasing countenance, speaks both French and English, about forty-five years of age." The slave bore the brand (applied by the previous owner) "S24" on his chest; he was said "to be lurking about the city of Savannah or Sapelo main."[17]

There is, then, no way to take a clear measure of the psychological stress of either the terrified slaves newly from Africa and unable to comprehend what was being done to them or the veterans who knew—in at least two languages—all too well. But we can make out the contours of the unusual structure of the Sapelo communities. The new slaves were young: "vessels seldom shipped 'merchandise' younger than fifteen, or older than twenty-three or twenty-four." After 1810, Spalding allegedly bought no slaves; he didn't need to: "plantation books in 1840 and 1851 used to show for four hundred souls annual births of sixty, seventy and eighty; death, five, six and seven." By the time he made his last will, he had "given to my two sons and four married daughters over one thousand negroes."[18]

Thomas Spalding sought in "the management of slave property—to make them a serf peasantry."[19] He did so perhaps in part to work past his great-grandfather's passionate demand that there never be slavery in Georgia. In 1738, "John Mackintosh Moore" and seventeen other residents of "New Inverness" (Darien) petitioned Governor James E. Oglethorpe to reject the request of "our Neighbors of Savannah . . . for the Liberty of having Slavery." To no avail, these Scotsmen wrote: "It's shocking to human Nature, that any Race of Mankind, and their Posterity, should be sentenced to perpetual Slavery; nor in Justice can we think otherwise of it, than they are thrown amongst us to be our Scourge one Day or another for our Sins; and as Freedom to them must be as dear as to us, what a Scene of Horror must it bring about! And the longer it be unexecuted, the bloody Scene must be the greater."[20]

If this echo from his mother's family sounded in his conscience we do not know; more surely, Thomas Spalding, with his sense of being responsible for a structured hierarchical society, found it comfortable to think of his slaves as serfs. This antique antidemocratic doctrine he made square with his concepts of a modern, scientific agricultural enterprise. On his domain, he sought to establish "a peonage belonging to the soil and the family."[21] In this, in part, he and they succeeded. The Sapelo people still hold to place and family.

In writing of the feeding of newcomers, Wylly reported that they were fed from barns, not from one barn. Similarly, a contributing factor to the high birthrate was "a division of the families into settlements or villages."[22] Beginning as a safe and orderly way of introducing slaves onto his remote island, Spalding encouraged family formation in family-oriented villages, the hammocks. Newly arrived slaves were assigned to a strong disciplined man or woman and under that tutelage brought into the village. These family villages remain today in the memory of the hammocks now left behind, and in the churches, the First African Baptist, which was moved from Raccoon Bluff, and St. Luke's, founded in 1884 in Hog Hammock. People move freely from one church to another in the alternately scheduled services, but it is still true that Julius Bailey and the Carters, Hillerys, and Dixons are St. Luke's; the Greens, Bankses, and Cornelia Bailey are First African Baptist.

Whatever the toll on the newly arrived slaves, on those who were required to train them (and who elected to comfort them)—on people enslaved, Spalding's scheme engendered a sense of community solidarity that is still in place. It is nearly two hundred years since Africans fierce with grief made their hammocks their own. There the wild African tribe made of itself a people. A people visible; coming up on the Meridian dock there can be no mistaking a person's belonging. The mark is there in the set of the jaw and the weight of the head, in the stature and gait of the old men as they take their seats on either of the church's deacon's bench, in Cornelia Walker Bailey as she strides up the gangway.

But color even more than physical structure is Sapelo's true ensign. It is distinctive, even unique. It is theirs. Argene Grovner, eight generations from Africa, is its Rembrandt canvas; the boatman's face outdoes Nathaniel Jocelyn's *Cinque* and Thomas Eakin's *Negress*; his is our most richly colored American face. A brush would want a daub from almost every pigment on the pallet to do justice to his rich burnish of brown, blue-black, red, and gold. Grovner's forehead, turned to the light as he deftly tends to the lines that make the boat secure, is a magnificent banner of defiant African memory.

5

Marsh Landing

Yesterday afternoon, I walked for miles on woods roads on the island's east side. I was lonely and getting weary; the moss beards on the oaks were coming close to being tiresome clichés; I'd seen the tall pines before. The slurp and loud splash of something—a turtle? an alligator?—plunging into the torpid water behind the brush along the right side of the trail startled me back into curiosity. The trees were behind me now, the thicket of brush left off, and I was out on the short stretch of low, oyster-white dunes as the sun struck. Before me was the whole ocean; to either side the beach, flatter than any other I know, seemed to stretch as endlessly as the sea.

I was alone. No person, no structure was there. Nothing intruded. Behind the dunes, sun-bleached to an intense white, there was only a distant, low fringe of trees back across the salt marsh. In front was an emptiness of outrageous beauty, and I heard my own voice give a gasp of delight. I'm not sure I know what an epiphany is, but only once or twice in my life have I felt as I did at that moment. And happily talking to myself now, this unbeliever suddenly said, "I will lift up mine eyes unto the hills." No hills anywhere around, but those were the words that came out. "Whence cometh my help?" I laughed at myself as that tumbled out of me; help doesn't come from any whence, but it's there in those dunes, that beach slanting to the ocean.

I couldn't possibly use such fancy language to talk to anyone about that seemingly endless stretch of the world, but as I walk along its shore, I wonder if that ocean still mocks Hog Hammock. The sea was the highway of slavery and this coast its beaching. I have trouble imagining that any of Thomas Spalding's slaves experienced epiphanies out here on this beach. And yet, it would have been the right place for Bilali and his wife, Phoebe, to have prayed to the east.

We know that they spread their mats to pray; did they do their ritual washing before prayer here in the slow, calm surf after spreading their mats toward Mecca here on this flat gray-white pavement? Prayer is the only formal thought of which we have record for the island's slaves. How Bilali and Phoebe and other slaves felt about slavery has been teased out of many obscure sources, and much of our understanding has had to come from a taking apart of accounts by white observers who wrote about their black subjects from their own perspectives. My unoriginal hunch is that the Sapelo slaves thought poorly indeed of the discipline of their lives and spent little time wondering where, on a scale ranging from revolt to resignation, they stood. Thomas Spalding's biographer did make such assessments: "Occasionally slaves absconded—not many, for when a slave had been with him [Spalding] long enough to learn his plantation methods, he learned enough to want to stay."[1]

Apologists for Spalding were undoubtedly right that few alternatives open to a man or woman escaping would have been more bearable than slavery on Sapelo. Even if slaves were willing to take the chance that there might be, they couldn't go without leaving everyone caring and cared about. For a time, a slave might hide out in the tangle of one of the other, uninhabited islands, but want of food and fresh water would likely drive the person out; recapture along the nineteenth-century Georgia coast was almost certain.[2]

Running away and suicide were ways of taking fate in one's own hands, but only in desperation, and in one case momentarily, in the other with terrible finality. And the freedom to make either of those choices diminished as the slaves ceased to be a parcel of strangers and became a people depending on one another. A person was responsible for others as well as self. To flee was to be caught and punished—very likely by sale away from where you had made trouble and from the only people you knew; to kill yourself was to abandon a family as much as did the man or woman who took flight.

What was left to do was to struggle to alleviate the worst of slavery in your private time in your hammock. Life there in that slave community might, despite the odds, be made rich, but you and your neighbors could effect little fundamental improvement in your situation. The chance to take full charge of your life did not exist.

That chance was to come as the result of a war, but before the moment came, that war was to make the lot of Sapelo's people worse than it had been. And yet, from the start, it raised hopes. They knew that the war had something to do with them. There is no record of how informed they were about political events in the nation as the arguments intensified over the retention or abolition of their slavery. There would have been plenty of gossip to listen to in Randolph Spalding's big south-end house, which he had inherited from his father, or at Duplin on the west side of the island, where his sister, Catherine Spalding Kenan, lived. (They and their four mainland siblings had, between them, received their father's one thousand slaves following his death.) Randolph Spalding, unlike his scientific father, better fit the popular image of the Southern plantation grandee; in his thirties as the war approached, he liked fast horses and big house parties. When white people came to visit, black people picked up news.

In the fall and winter of 1860–61, the news was secession. South Carolina left the Union in December, Georgia in January; by the first of February all of the states of the deep South had followed suit. Months before any act of war, fears were great of a "plundering expedition" aimed at the huge population of slaves along the coast. Charles Spalding, Randolph's brother, wrote to an offical of the Georgia militia on February 11 "that there are on the Island of Sapelo . . . about five hundred negroes which might be swept off any day unless protected by a small detachment of infantry on the island." Spalding feared not only slave raiders, but the slaves themselves: "there are on . . . [the nearby Altamaha rice plantations] some four thousand negroes, whose owners will continue to feel very insecure until some naval defenders are placed upon these waters."[3]

Spalding's fears were warranted. Although the war that began in April 1861 with the firing on Fort Sumter left the region for a time, it came back to Sapelo and the other sea islands sooner than it was to return to any other part of the deep South. To block entrance of supplies to Charleston and Savannah, the Union Navy seized the sea island harbor of Port Royal in South Carolina in November 1861. (Randolph Spalding, a colonel now in the Confederate Army, was to have led his regiment in what proved to be a futile defense of Port Royal, but, to the dismay of some of his fellow planters, was too drunk to do so—or so ran the gossip.)[4] Ships then ranged undeterred along the Georgia islands, and white Georgians in the port of Darien talked openly of their fear that the Yankees would take their town and turn the slaves loose.

The slaves were intrigued by that idea and intensely curious about what was going on. Those on one island kept in close touch with their fellows on other islands— and the mainland—even though the islands are not close and communication between them not easy. A fishing boat slipping from one island's wharf to another's, a slave sent on an errand to the mainland overhearing white people (who were talking of little else but the war), provided tantalizing news. When slaves sighted a naval ship off the coast they knew something—something important—was going on.

Their masters knew so too. With federal ships not only in Port Royal harbor but standing off Sapelo itself, with federal troops commandeering the houses of planters like themselves up in Beaufort, with goddam abolitionists already swarming over the islands stirring up "our people," and with raiding parties coming onto the islands around Savannah's harbor fifty miles to the north, Mary Bass Spalding was determined to get out of the way.[5] Since her husband was off at the war, the plans to leave were in her hands and in those of her sister-in-law, Catherine Spalding Kenan, and her husband, Michael J. Kenan.

Unlike simpler McIntosh County neighbors who, with nowhere else to go and no desire to leave home, formed a militia company to defend the coast, Mary Spalding had Bass relatives with landholdings in Baldwin County large enough to accommodate the hundreds of slaves she planned to take with her. Michael Kenan was also from Baldwin County, well up in the interior of the state, where his family owned two large plantations.[6]

Surprisingly, no account of the exodus exists, but it is clear that Baldwin County was where they went. Half a century later, Randolph Spalding's daughter-in-law recalled that the slaves "had been moved, en masse, to a rented plantation . . . near Milledgeville, when the family refugeed to that place."[7] And a descendant of one slave couple, Boson and Phyllis Gardner, who were married there in 1863, had Milledgeville firmly in her memory.[8] (Milledgeville was the state capital; the larger town of Macon was nearby.)

The Spalding heirs could not take their thousands of acres, but were determined to take their other assets, their slaves. Some of the slaves were even more determined not to be taken. Charles Hall, long the storekeeper on Sapelo, recalled tales from just before he was born: "Slaves hiding in the marshes watched out for Yankee boats and informed island negroes when boats were in the waterways."[9] Hall named eight Sapelo men who got onto those boats and joined the Union Army: "Mars Carter, Sam Robert, Jim Walker (who fought under the name of James Spalding, the son of old man Charles Spalding), Peter Maxwell, . . . Mart Jackson, Fuller Wilson, Quatner Johnson, . . . and Mart Wilson." A ninth man, John Johnson, did not make it. He was "shot by the Master while attempting a running escape toward a waiting Yankee boat."[10]

The Spaldings and Kenans had to move quickly (or use their guns often) if those Union ships were not to have still more passengers. Orchestrating the move cannot have been easy, although the family may have had the help of a detachment of militia. There is no account of the leave-taking from Marsh Landing, but there are vivid scraps of memory. Katie Brown recalled long afterward what she wore: The master's record of her young age was in error; she was old enough to wear a shift rather than the usual child's garment, an empty flour sack with slits cut through it for head and arms.[11]

To transport lumber and the numerous bales of their annual cotton crop to the mainland, the Spaldings would have owned both large, broad-beamed sailboats with their masts well forward and out of the cargo's way and long, wide, several-oared skiffs in which slaves ferried goods. Thirty to fifty people, with all of the possessions allowed them bundled into a knotted rag, could have crowded into a sailboat, ten in a skiff. My guess is that at least three hundred Sapelo people were taken to the mainland this way.

Aboard, too, were surely some of the white families' household goods, provisions for the trip, probably some farm animals, and almost certainly horses to mount and

to draw the family carriages. Once everything and everyone was at the Meridian dock, the refugees would have
begun the trek of close to two hundred miles inland. Catherine, Mary, and Mary's seventeen-year-old daughter and
ten-year-old son in a carriage in the charge of slave coach-
men would have led the way. The only male family adult,
Michael Kenan, and perhaps fourteen-year-old Thomas
Spalding, along with overseers, would have followed at
the rear to prevent any of the people—the better than
$300,000 in assets—on their forced march from dropping
off into the scraps of forest along the route.

Most of the country through which they moved was
cleared for farming and still under the well-disciplined
peacetime order of slavery. The sight of planters leading
bands of slaves away from overworked Georgia lands to
try again in Alabama or Texas—in the West—made this
exodus not unique. But the dusty Sapelo people, probably
chanting as they struggled forward, would have been the
first doleful signal to both black and white people along
the way of what lay ahead in the war. They did not know
it then, but a good many of them were also going to be
war refugees along these same roads.

Scores and scores of Sapelo's people made this trek, but
the Spaldings and Kenans had left some behind. Those
left were the oldest, those who could remember the agony
of other forced separations. The records of the families
living on the island today reveal that eight of their forebears were over seventy and some close to a hundred in
1861. And these would by no means have been the only
old people who were deserted. There would have been
little point in the Spaldings' taking other than able-bodied
slaves with them, little likelihood that the eldest of them
would survive the walking. It is possible that some weaned

children too large to carry and too small for the long walk may also have been left behind.

A young surgeon in the Union Navy wrote in his diary on February 20, 1863: "Took a tramp in the interior of Sapelo Island. After traveling six miles through swamps, briars, etc., we arrived at an old hut inhabited by 7 super-annuated contrabands [the earliest term for the former slaves] and one cripple—all poor as Job's turkey. From them I learned that a man by the name of Randolph Spalding used to live on this island. . . . He was in possession of 300 darkies ere the war, but they have been removed to the mainland."[12]

The surgeon did not know that some able-bodied Africans had not been removed. March Wilson, for one, had made his way north—as far as Port Royal Island, South Carolina, to enlist, on December 2, 1862, in the First South Carolina Volunteers, the first Union regiment composed of former slaves. Later, as the army began making room for 200,000 black soldiers, the regiment was renamed the 33rd Regiment of the United States Colored Volunteers. Wilson was in Company B; his colonel was Thomas Wentworth Higginson.

Higginson, before coming south to command the black regiment, had been a Unitarian minister and radical abolitionist. Now, for the first time, he was confronting black men who had been slaves. On the day that March Wilson enlisted, Higginson noted in his diary that recruitment was difficult because his predecessor, General David Hunter, had originally raised the regiment as if he had been moving slaves from one task to another. The men were not volunteers; they were, in effect, drafted. Recruitment would have been "rapid," wrote Higginson, "were it not for the legacy of bitter distrust bequeathed" by that earlier "abortive" attempt to raise a black regiment, "into which [the recruits] were driven like cattle, kept for several months in camp, and then turned off without a shilling."[13]

March Wilson was welcomed with a promise that he would be treated with respect as a soldier and given pay. But he was told by black neighbors of the camp that he couldn't count on the latter. When the colonel published his diary, he added this footnote: "With what utter humiliation were we, their officers, obliged to confess to them, eighteen months afterwards, that it was their distrust that was wise, and our faith in the United States Government which was foolishness!"[14]

Higginson did treat his men with respect, in part because he was so much enjoying the experience of living with them in an army camp in a luxurious climate: " 'Dwelling in tents with Abraham, Isaac, and Jacob,' this condition is certainly mine,—and with a multitude of patriarchs beside, not to mention Caesar and Pompey, Hercules and Bacchus." The colonel lived in two wall tents joined as one; March Wilson shared his smaller slant-sided tent with Richard Robinson from Darien and April Coen from nearby Liberty County.

The Unitarian preacher-colonel was astonished by the pervasiveness of Christianity in the lives of his soldiers, a faith to which they had given their own—to him—mysterious slant: "One of their favorite songs is full of plaintive cadences; it is not, I think, a Methodist tune, and I wonder where they obtained a chant of such beauty.

'I can't stay behind, my Lord, I can't stay behind!
O, my father is gone, my father is gone,

My father is gone into heaven, my Lord!
  I can't stay behind!
Dere's room enough, room enough,
Dere's room enough in de heaven for de sojer: Can't stay
  behind!' "[15]

Higginson listened to his men and recorded their prayers: "I hab lef' my wife in de land o' bondage: my little
ones dey say eb'ry night, Whar is my fader? But when I
die, when de bressed mornin' rises, when I shall stan' in
de glory, wid one foot on de water an' one foot on de
land, den, O Lord, I shall see my wife an' my little chil'en
once more."[16]

If the Yankee colonel took a patronizing tone in
describing these Southerners, he did observe them closely
and intelligently, and they taught him lessons decades in
a Northern pulpit could not have taught. And if he had a
sharp eye out, so did they. On Edisto, an island very like
Sapelo, where the regiment was encamped, the black
recruits had the pleasure of watching the Unitarian
preacher-colonel being seduced by the South he had come
to liberate. Nowhere in American sports literature is there
a more sensuous rendition of a swim than Higginson's
account in *Army Life in a Black Regiment*: "The tide was
well up, though still on the flood, as I desired; and each
visible tuft of marsh grass might, but for its motionless,
have been a prowling boat. Dark as the night had
appeared, the water was pale, smooth, and phosphores-
cent. . . . it was a warm, breathless Southern night. There
was no sound but the faint swash of the coming tide, the
noises of the reedbirds in the marshes, and the occasional
leap of a fish. . . ."[17]

Higginson was curious about the waterways cutting into the rebel shore—what size boats they could accommodate; he had been given conflicting information—but reconnaissance was more an excuse than not: "I do not remember ever to have experienced a greater sense of exhilaration than when I slipped noiselessly into the placid water, and struck out into the smooth, eddying current for the opposite shore. The night was so still and lovely, my black statues looked so dream-like at their posts behind the low earthwork, the opposite arm of the causeway stretched so invitingly from the Rebel main, the horizon glimmered so low around me . . . that I seemed floating in some concave globe, some magic crystal, of which I was the enchanted centre."[18]

On the way across, Higginson disciplined himself not to fear Glasco Bailey's sharks, but the expert swimmer imagined himself creating "a splashing . . . loud enough to be heard at Richmond,"[19] and his head seemed to grow into a gigantic target that he could not obscure. Despite the ominous barking of a dog, he went undetected and did learn the way the waterways cut into the rebel shore. Then, as he turned back, he found that the tide had turned. He lost sight of his own causeway: "As I swam steadily, but with some sense of fatigue . . . everything seemed to shift and waver, in the uncertain light. The distant trees seemed not trees, but bushes, and the bushes might not exactly be but bushes, but might after all, be distant trees." Suddenly "I felt a sensation of fine ribbons drawn softly across my person"; it was not some sea creature, but rushes that marked not the shore, but the first of a series of unfamiliar small tidal islands. Beating back panic and "that awful sensation of having one's foot

unsupported, which benumbs the spent swimmer's heart,"
he turned on his back and glided the final stretch into
shore—to hear: "Halt! Who's go dar?"

" 'F-f-friend with the c-c-countersign,' retorted I, with
a chilly but conciliatory energy, rising at full length out of
the shallow water, to show myself a man and a brother.
. . . And there as I stood, a dripping ghost, . . . the
unconscionable fellow . . . deliberately presented arms!"[20]
Whether that sentry was March Wilson or Sam Roberts or
whoever he was, it isn't hard to imagine the belly laughs
later that night as black men rolled round in their tents
imagining that stark naked, dripping, lunatic white boy,
correctly (and safely) stammering out the password in his
weird Yankee voice.

Higginson's Sapelo privates no doubt thought him a
damned fool for going on such an exploit, but a nice,
reliable fool. And they were with him from their first
armed expedition, the retaking of Jacksonville, Florida,
south of the last of the Georgia islands, on March 10,
1863, just over two months after the signing of the Emancipation Proclamation. Sapelo soldiers sailed past their
island on their way south and past it again when their
company joined the expedition in which the Massachusetts 54th made its famous failed July 1863 assault on Fort
Wagner, on Morris Island, guarding the Charleston harbor. Early in 1865, when Sherman's huge armies, having
camped on the sea islands, set out to take the Carolinas,
March's company joined them, but the truth be told, we
cannot be sure March was with them.

"I was with my company all the time," Wilson reported
on a pension application forty years after the war. He was
mustered out from Morris Island at the war's end, then it

was back to Sapelo: "I was born on this island, the slave of Thomas Spaulding and remained his slave until freedom," a freedom he had fought to secure. He came back to his island, as did the white Spaldings—"His [Thomas Spalding's] granddaughter Mrs. McKinley is P[ost] M[istress] here now." But that was long after the war, and a pension was at stake. In fact, Wilson's statement "I was with my company all the time" does not square with the record.[21]

Wilson's service record shows that he "was absent in desertion from August 28, 1863, to September [or October] 2, 1864." He "surrendered from desertion," in the fall of 1864, was held "in confinement awaiting trial," and restored to duty, without trial, in April 1865. A cryptic comment on the jacket of his record suggests that "conditions" of the desertion were mitigating; like many other privates, black and white, he may have found word of privation at home more compelling than the sometimes listless duty in the service; March almost surely had gone home. His desertion, as the war ended, apparently did not seem culpable to the officers of his regiment; one noted on his record, "The charge of desertion no longer stands against him."[22]

The Union fleet was busy along the Georgia coast doing more than transporting troops. From the fall of 1861 on, sailors not only had to keep blockade runners out of the major harbors of Charleston and Savannah, but had to deny them entry to the mainland on other channels. Large ships had long carried lumber from the Georgia ports of Brunswick and Darien, towns that would have made good places to land Confederate supplies. But the waterways to those towns were only two of dozens which needed patrolling. Naval ships came as well into Doboy Sound to the south of Sapelo, where a channel reaching and reversing leads on long slants into the two-wharf port of Meridian.

I know that stretch of water some. Five-thirty on a December evening, Caesar Banks—on this trip, I'm staying with him and his wife, Nancy—and I have gone down to meet the five-fifteen boat from Meridian; we stand, alone, waiting, at Marsh Landing, on a planked dock thrust out into the harbor. Doboy Sound is magic in its beauty. Pink-orange stripes—the last light of the gone-down sun—reach like pale searchlights low over small islands jutting on the southwestward horizon, throwing slashes of color into the dark water. That water is rushing toward us to complete the rising tide.

Directly above us, a dark cloud bank is breaking up. The clean, backward C of the moon keeps coming into view and slipping away. To the northwest, beyond the islands of spartina grass on the other side of the channel, the wheelhouse lights of a boat headed south on the Intracoastal Waterway make their slow transit. Back over our left shoulder, bearing a single white light, a homecoming shrimp boat inches in on its way from the ocean and finds its own path through the marsh to its dock in nearby Valona. Finally, out of the tricky channel, the *Sapelo Queen* is in sight.

She reaches away from us for a moment to line up with the buoys, turns sharply to port, and coming close to the dock, flips back on her own wake and grazes the pilings. With two lines, the crewman, Argene Grovner, makes the boat secure.

The wharf, sun-scorched at midday, is now a cool

white in the electric light suddenly beamed toward the *Sapelo Queen*. Grovner lugs the gangway into place and the half-dozen passengers slant their way toward us. The last of them is Allen Green, his twisted legs impeding him not a bit as he drags a heavy sack of rice. Unobtrusively, Caesar hurries down to shoulder the bag and toss it into the back of Allen Green's pickup.

An unlikely greeter, I shake Allen Green's soft, enfolding, impressively strong and welcoming hand. He recognizes me right away; he had spotted me from the deacon's bench in St. Luke's[23] the day before and recollected conversations we had had on an earlier trip of mine to Sapelo. Then, we had sat on the porch of his small trim house close to the northernmost reach of Hog Hammock.

In the light sun on that earlier morning, Allen Green and I were moving almost imperceptibly on his narrow porch swing, I on his right. Elbows bent, his right arm and my left lay over the swing's back as I leaned round toward him to position my good right ear to try to hear clearly his rapid-fire Gullah-inflected voice. Concentrating on a story, I found myself staring at his hand—and at mine; they were not two inches apart.

Never before had I been as conscious of my hand's color—brown age-freckles on blurry cream. Allen Green's hand, not large, but molded as by a sculptor with mounds of strength in its back and fingers, has for seventy-seven years shaped some of the most delicate, artistic baskets on the Georgia coast. And looking at our two hands—my mind wandering now from his almost incomprehensible story—I found myself pondering matters of race, of color.

What in hell has the blue chestnut-brown of Green's hand and the mottled off-white of mine had to do with all

the idiotic hatred that has plagued the whole of our land—
and the immediate land of Hog Hammock—for the last
two or three hundred years? Am I the typical academic
"white" man trying to overcome my physical inferiority
by imposing, in some quirky academic way, my superior
European will on this naturally superior "black" African
man? Or is this the bullshit I know it to be? What's hap-
pening is that two men, reaching to get acquainted, both
of whom have been battered (in exceedingly different
ways) by a lot of American years, are sitting on a porch
swing.

Those hands of ours are close in another way. They are
the tools each of us uses to say what we can about our
world. He uses his to make baskets that merit the place
they have won in museums; I put my hands to work on a
keyboard to say in books what I would like to be able to
say to Allen Green as we sit on the porch swing. I don't
trust knowing what I think until my hands have gotten the
words on paper. And here on Green's porch, much of
what comes out of my rattletrap out-of-Manhattan voice
is as incomprehensible to Green as his half-Gullah stories
often are to me.

Try as I do to turn Allen Green into a narrative historian, I don't succeed. The past is all snapshots; he was, as
he had told me without connecting events into a story,
taught basketmaking by his grandfather—"Named for
my grandfather"—"Came from Macon; Sapelo after slavery. . . ." A chronicle of that odyssey doesn't flow from
him. Instead, his imagination reaches into the past as if
each event were like his photograph in the living room
standing next to Jimmy Carter in 1979 when the president
attended the Easter service at Deacon Green's First Afri-

can Baptist Church across the road. History for Allen Green consists of moments, of pieces of the past.

The chronicle of Allen Green's grandfather Allen Smith during the Civil War doesn't seem to interest him as much as it does me. But he knows his facts. When, finally, he does make it clear that Allen Smith was Bilally Smith's son—and that Bilally Smith was, in turn, Bilali's grandson—I am pretty sure that I know at least three of the slaves that were ferried from the island early in the war.[24] Twenty-six-year-old Allen Smith, his fifty-year-old father, and his mother, in her early forties, were among the Sapelo people who were taken away from their island, taken, perhaps, from the same Marsh Landing, off Doboy Sound, where, on that haunting evening, I had watched Allen Green come home.

Just over a year after the Civil War exodus, in February 1863, the barque S.S. *Fernandina* and the gunboat S.S. *Wamsutta* were on blockade duty in Doboy Sound. In June the waters between Sapelo and St. Simons contained a good many Union ships, including those which transported the Massachusetts 54th for its raid on Darien: "The sight was beautiful. Whether it was proper and pat to burn the place I know not," wrote Samuel P. Boyer, a young naval surgeon, "but I do know the place was reduced to ashes."[25] He added that, prior to the torching of the "beautiful, flourishing, and striving town," he had gone ashore on Sapelo and found it not in all ways inviting: "Of all the places in the States I think that Sapelo Island, Ga. is the greatest place for snakes, for no less than one hundred have been seen this season," and the "venomous" mosquitoes "arrive in clouds from the marshes like volumes of dust in the deserts of Arabia. . . . Blood is their cry."[26]

Boyer found the wide, flat beach irresistible—"Took a run on shore"—and, turning inland, discovered that some of the people living on Sapelo had established a profitable wartime enterprise.[27] Some abandoned Spalding slaves, joined, almost surely, by some of the thousands of slaves who throughout the war ran away from inland plantations to find refuge on the islands free of white people, were farming. The physician had time for exploring and running, because he had few patients: "Having plenty of fresh beef and vegetables, which we obtained on Sapelo, the ship's company cannot help being healthy."[28]

His fellow naval officers were kept well informed. They were regularly receiving news of the Confederate port of Savannah by reading the *Savannah Morning News*. One Confederate resident of McIntosh County reported that "among the Negroes who were daily leaving their owners, there were several sensible fellows who robbed their masters' mail before they left. They took with them all late pieces of mail."[29] Information gathered from both posted circulars and private correspondence and from overheard conversation was transmitted, along with the newspapers.

Slaves breaking for it were proving to be some of the War of the Rebellion's best rebels. The sea islands of South Carolina and Georgia experienced the arrival of a constant stream of people who had fled their masters, and Sapelo was not exempt. One of the Spalding family members lamented that the island "was taken possession of by vagrant runaway negroes and held by them during the war."[30] No names were given, but at least some of these vagrants (a favorite term the world over for ex-slaves seeking to create new ways of life for themselves after emancipations) were not strangers, but, instead, Spalding slaves who had escaped—and gone home.

One of these people was Jane Cummings Lemon. In May 1865, Corporal James Lemon persuaded his captain, N. G. Parker, to request for him a furlough of "fifteen days to visit his family, at Sapelo Island. When this man joined the service he left his wife in slavery. She has since escaped and is now at the latter place in a destitute condition. The Corporal desires to visit her to provide for her necessities." Lieutenant Colonel C. T. Trowbridge had enrolled the escaped "boatman," from "Sapelo Isl, Ga," on St. Catherines Island, fifteen miles to the north, on November 5, 1862. Now, simply, he wrote: "Approved—Corporal Lemon is particularly deserving."[31]

Not only had Jane Cummings Lemon escaped and gotten back to Sapelo, she had brought with her the couple's four children, ranging in age from five to fifteen. When his father escaped to join the Union Army, the youngest, Abram Lemon, was only a year old. That Captain Parker used the word "escaped" and the phrase "and is now" on Sapelo firmly suggests that Jane Lemon had been one of the slaves forced to go inland with the Spaldings; the "destitute condition" attests to the lot of those who escaped and moved coastward as refugees.

There is, however, no testimony to the anguish of the parting of husband and wife and children when he had gone off to join the Union Army. It is immensely difficult to ascertain how it was that so very many black men left their wives to join the Union Army. On one level it suggests a kind of male insensitivity to the often terrible burdens left to the women; on another, it points to the importance both men and women attached to the fight for freedom. Affectionate letters that remain suggest a mutual decision.

James Lemon almost certainly would have lost all contact with his wife and children when she and the children were taken into the interior of Georgia. Now someone from the island had gotten word to him that Jane and the children were back. That out of sight was decidedly not out of mind is demonstrated not only by the nature of James's request for a furlough but by the resumption of a marriage that was to last until his death in 1894. The Lemons had four more children after the war, and some of the fortitude the parents displayed during that conflict seems to have carried into the rearing of those children.

Thomas Lemon, the youngest of Jane and James Lemon's children, was the father of perhaps the most remarkable of Sapelo's people. Elizabeth Elaine Lemon's life could stand next to those of Benjamin Franklin and Frederick Douglass. Born on this remote island, she attended its grammar school only through the fourth grade and then boarded in Brunswick to attend St. Athanasius Episcopal School—"I was working to send myself to school since I was in the fifth grade"—and graduated from its high school with honors.

On the way to Atlanta University, "my shoes wore out. . . . The soles went completely and the outer rim spread like a moccasin's mouth! When students made fun of my feet, I held my head high and craned my neck to peer into the distance to see what was giving them so much fun." In that city university, she became the salutatorian of her normal school class. She went next to Ball State University in Indiana for her bachelor's degree in 1930, and, now a long, long way from home, to New York to earn a master's degree from Columbia.

Elizabeth Lemon taught first in Winston-Salem, North Carolina, and "went to New York each summer and joined up with a family that was spending the summer in the country. I . . . received higher wages than I was getting teaching. . . . I bought clothes, shoes, hats, luggage, and silk underwear and sent money home to Sapelo, as much as forty dollars at a time. I paid for [her younger sister] Kate's sewing lessons and was even saving toward a home one of these days."[32]

From 1930 to 1943, Lemon was the principal of Atlanta University's laboratory school (and taught Martin Luther King, Jr.) and later was the principal of the Frederick Douglass school in Gary, Indiana, where she proved to be a highly imaginative, inspiring teacher. No civic betterment activity escaped her, and on her retirement she traveled—on five continents—for the Young Men's Christian Association World Ambassadors.[33] Jane and James Lemon's granddaughter had gone a long way.

In November 1864, the false security that the Spaldings had achieved in Baldwin County was shattered by General William Tecumseh Sherman's immense army on its way from Atlanta to the sea. On November 22, his men took Milledgeville; on the 24th they moved toward the southeast across Baldwin County. The Sapelo people whom the Spaldings had sought to keep out of the way were right in the path of one of the most famous acts of wartime destruction. Left behind Sherman's march were chimneys bare of their houses and wrenched lives. To a large degree, the Confederate Army, apart from making harassing raids on Sherman's flanks, stayed out of harm's way. The sufferers were the civilians—black and white.

In the terrible confusion of burned cabins and desolated terrain, the people—the freed people, as the better-disposed federal soldiers had told them they now were—had to decide for themselves whether to go or stay. If it is remarkable that so many members of the families that had been taken to Baldwin County stayed together and made it back to Sapelo, it should not be forgotten that many more did not. Families fractured as people became desperate refugees. And yet, in grim circumstances, these people, for the first time in their lives, were making their own decisions. Their great chance had come to them in the midst of war.

6

Coming Home

Sapelo's people seized the chance. But not all in the same
way. Even after William Tecumseh Sherman's troops
smashed into their lives in central Georgia, some stayed
on in Baldwin County, while others moved away to the
north, south, and west. There are descendants of Sapelo
slaves living in Thomasville, Georgia, close to the Florida
border, a good distance south of Milledgeville. There are,
no doubt, others still living nearer the old Georgia capital:
"A great many people never did come back to Sapelo,"
recalled a descendant of those who did.[1] Returning, they
walked east—southeast—toward home.

Why? Why would people who had been forced to work
land as slaves ever want to see that dirt again? They were
free now from those who had done that forcing; why did
they go back to the scene of the crime? The clue to the
mystery lies in the fact that the memory of the scene was
as strong as that of the crime. The Sapelo people who
went back saw the place as separable from the oppression
that had taken place there.

So many of them had left the island that they couldn't be assured that the hammocks where family and neighbors had sustained one another would still be in place. But they couldn't let that stop them from going back to relatives they hoped had survived being left behind. They knew no other place as home. And I suspect there was another still more personal lure. After all, on that same island where they had been chattel slaves, they knew curtains of trees through which slipped secret paths to favorite fishing spots.

Their contemporary, Henry David Thoreau, who might be thought to have lived on another planet, pursued his privileged dissent from the crimes of this world in just such a way. His was not an escape to some exotic place, but an engagement—a walk in the local woods, where he could confront what troubled him. Without *Walden* to instruct them, slaves seem to have mastered his message; on a Sunday of one's own, away from any mastery, a person could take responsibility for himself or herself—could gather a peck of oysters from a creek bank no one else had discovered.

For Fortune Bell, for Sampson Hogg, a yearning to put their feet down on familiar ground appears to have been a compelling order to go home. Shad Hall, Sampson Hogg's son—having given their name to Hog Hammock, the family changed its name to Hall long after the war—became, six decades later, one of the best chroniclers of Sapelo's history. He once described for his great-nephew how his father had followed Sherman's army. (Shad himself may have been one of the children left on Sapelo; he was about eight when the Spaldings marched their adult slaves inland and did not include himself in the tale of the trek.) Leaving the same day the army moved through, Sampson Hogg would have left Milledgeville on November 24, 1864. A week later and one hundred miles farther, he would have been at Millen, halfway to the coast.

By now, there were 25,000 freedpeople following 57,000 Union soldiers marching in four columns, two under General O. O. Howard on the right and two, on the left, under General Henry W. Slocum, with whom Sherman rode.[2] This left flank was the one that had taken Milledgeville, freeing the slaves concentrated there. We do not know precisely which plantation they had been living on or, immediately, what happened to the Spalding families that had brought them there. They, no doubt, got quickly out of Sherman's way, probably heading for the homes of still other relatives farther to the north and out of the Union Army's path.

Nor do we know the condition of the quarters in which the Sapelo slaves had been living after the traversal of the soldiers in the march to the sea, which, as Sherman put it, left "a devastation more or less relentless."[3] Behind the soldiers, and often more capriciously vicious, were foragers—some desperate refugees, others callous looters— committing "many acts of pillage, robbery, and violence."[4] There is every reason to believe that the destruction in Baldwin County was sufficient to discourage many Sapelo people from staying.

There was also the hope that their island could be reclaimed. Unlike their ancestors brought across an ocean, they could go home on foot. But theirs was no triumphant journey. Freedom, for the moment, meant being a war refugee. You walked as long as you had the strength to keep going; when members of the family faltered, someone had to decide whether the rest should stop or go on, carrying infants and old people too weak to walk. On their backs and in their hands were food, clothing, and covering to ward off the cold of fall nights spent sleeping on the ground—nights shared with the fear of soldiers' violence.

This exodus was an arduous trek of close to two hundred miles—or more, depending on the route—on foot; a few farm wagons may have been taken to carry the infirm and mothers with babies, but there can't have been many vehicles. When whatever food they carried was gone, they were dependent on the foraging they could do. The pickings would have been slim; hungry soldiers ahead of them made a clean sweep of chickens and harvested corn. The roads hard, drinking water uncertain, and nights cold, these Georgians, along with a good many other Georgians, suffered the travails of centuries of war refugees the world round.

"The south deserves all she has got from her injustice to the Negro," declared Sherman, who, nonetheless, had "decided to rid himself of the problem"[5]—the vast throng of refugees following him. As he advanced on Savannah, he had reports that the Confederates had reinforced their positions at the now nearby city, and there were frequent glancing attacks on the Union columns. To these, the refugees were more vulnerable than the soldiers they followed.

The opportunity for one army corps to separate itself from the refugees came at Ebenezer Creek, a muddy,

swollen stream lying east of the Ogeechee River and flow-
ing into the Savannah River. Confederate cavalrymen
were known to be in the area, and Union general Jefferson
C. Davis ordered "his men ahead at the double quick and
left the blacks to the rear."[6] At the water's edge, the refugees were told that they were being restrained for their
own safety as there was fighting ahead; then, when the
last wagons following the troops had crossed, the pontoon
bridge was swiftly taken up. "There went up from that
multitude a cry of agony," reported a Union chaplain.[7]

Someone, a mocking soldier or a frightened refugee,
shouted "rebels," and the first of the five hundred frantic
people "stampeded with a rush into the icy water old and
young alike, men and women and children, swimmers
and nonswimmers, determined not to be left behind by
the deliverers they had supposed had come to lead them
out of bondage."[8] Some swam across, others, "several of
them women who carried babies in their arms . . . were
swept downstream and drowned."[9]

Contrite Union soldiers threw logs and timbers into the
stream, which, retrieved on the other side, were fashioned
into a raft by several of the black men. One of them, powerful enough to ford the stream and drag the raft after him,
crossed and recrossed rescuing those who could get
aboard. The threat of a Confederate attack proved accurate. A detachment of Confederate cavalry fired on the
civilians and drove those left on the bank back from the
stream, reportedly returning several to nearby former owners. Of General Davis, one Minnesota private wrote:
"Legree was an angel of mercy in comparison."[10]

The incident at Ebenezer Creek illustrates not only
how grim could be the lot of war refugees, but also the

determination of these particular people to escape the slavery in which they had been held. Many of the survivors who made it to the coast were total strangers to the region, and even the Sapelo people had no way of knowing exactly what point they would reach. Those following Howard's column reached the sea at Confederate Fort McAllister, where the Ogeechee River meets the tidal waters leading out to Osabaw Island, two islands north of Sapelo. When that fort, the last major defense of Savannah, fell, the road into the city was clear.

There was a victory to celebrate; the soldiers were winning these Southerners' war. Civil War histories are full of accounts of triumphant Union soldiers as Fort McAllister fell and the army connected with the navy carrying fresh rations and, better still, mail. But no accounts tell of the emotions of the others, those who looked again at familiar December-frosted marsh grass. If victory wasn't the word for what they had achieved, perhaps, deliverance was. They did not know what they had come back to, but now they knew where they were. These refugees were only thirty miles from Sapelo.

Sampson Hogg made it home, perhaps directly from Fort McAllister. More of the Sapelo people, along with tens of thousands of others, were in Savannah. Some had gotten there by following the armies which had moved into and around the port, others had found their way on their own. The islanders among this latter group would have arrived by groping their way. Remembrance of the march to Milledgeville, however vivid, would not have been sufficient to accomplish a repetition in reverse. That path would have been from crossroads to crossroads through remote and hostile country in search of Darien.

A safer, surer route led to Savannah along a main road and, from Dublin, along the railroad tracks east and then south into the city.

Savannah in the winter of 1864–65 was crowded with black refugees seeking shelter and food; temporarily, they more than doubled the little city's population. Simple survival was their task. In December and early January, General Sherman was also in the city—Savannah had been his Christmas present to President Lincoln. He denied reports both of refugees being driven away from his army and of their being murdered by marauding Confederate troops: "A cock and bull story."[11] But he complained that his army of sixty thousand was "overloaded with two-thirds negroes, five-sixths of whom are helpless, and a large proportion of them babies and small children."[12] Forty thousand refugees—or even close to that number—in a city with an 1860 population of 22,292 caused severe problems.

To dispose of them, the American most famous for his scorn of politics made a political decision of radical proportions. Sherman, responding to an immediate wartime need, engaged in what in the 1990s would be scorned, by some, as "social engineering." Like many other of Reconstruction's experiments, this one was largely erased from white America's historical memory as laissez-faire concepts of private property reasserted themselves soon after the war. But it did happen. Heeding the assurance of a delegation of black men who called on him (and to whom, to his credit, he listened) that their people would be happy to be left to their own devices, William Tecumseh Sherman ordered a massive—even socialistic—redistribution of land.

The general had a precedent to follow. On the sea islands of South Carolina, deserted by white planters on the arrival of Union forces in the fall of 1861, black workers, now free, had been farming family-size plots independently and successfully. General Rufus Saxton, in command of Union forces on the sea islands, was, by great good fortune, a true friend of the freed people and, as a kind of military governor, presided over the Port Royal Experiment. When the white planters abandoned their island plantations and their slaves, the latter established themselves as independent farmers. They had help from Gideon's Band, volunteers sponsored by various freedmen's aid societies who conducted schools and assisted the freed people with learning the everyday ropes of living no longer as slaves. They had also lent a hand as the freed people frustrated the efforts of other white Northerners to organize the island economy in a way that would have perpetuated gang labor; instead, the islanders had become subsistence farmers living and working in family units on individual plots of land.

Saxton, a West Point graduate and career military officer, was the antithesis of General Davis of Ebenezer Creek. Prodded by an idealistic father who was a great friend of George Ripley, the founder of the famous communal experiment Brook Farm, Saxton was determined that the freedpeople would succeed, not communally, but as independent farmers. That he was also a West Pointer did the freed people no harm; General Sherman was able to stomach do-gooder actions when done by regular army men that he would have snorted at if done by the political generals he despised.

When the delegation of black men told the general that

they would prefer to be left alone and that they would not be dependent on his army, it was with the knowledge of the success of the Carolina sea islanders. It was they who provided the commander with a solution to his problem. If given land that they could farm, the refugees would stop following him. On January 16, 1865, the general issued Special Field Order 15: "The islands from Charleston south, the abandoned rice-fields along the rivers for thirty miles back from the sea, and the country bordering the St. John's River, Florida, are reserved and set apart for the settlement of the negroes now made free by the acts of war. . . ."[13]

Sapelo was safely centered in this large stretch of territory in which the people were to be on their own: "On the islands, and in the settlements hereafter to be established, no white person whatever, unless military officers and soldiers detailed for duty, will be permitted to reside; and the sole and exclusive management of affairs will be left to the freed people themselves."[14]

In the spring of 1865, with more slavery and war on their backs than anyone should have to endure, the refugees in Savannah had had enough of white folk. And yet, white folk were still doing for them. Fortunately, General Saxton was one of them; as Sherman's armies moved north into the Carolinas, Saxton was left behind to serve as, in effect, the military governor of Sherman's coastal maroon.

He and his staff were soon busy trying to relocate as many as possible of the thousands of Savannah refugees to the islands. Efficiently putting the reverse side of absconded Farmers and Mechanics Bank blank loan forms to use, they responded to requests from heads of house-

holds. Here is an example of one of the many warrants
neatly printed (in large quantities); the words in italics
were filled in by hand by the issuing officer.

To Whom It May Concern

Savannah, Ga *April 16* 1865

Fergus Wilson having selected for settlement *forty* Acres of
Land on *Sapelo Island Spaulding plant'n Ga* pursuant to
Special Field Order No. 15, Headquarters Military District
of Mississippi [the technical name of Sherman's command],
Jan. 16, 1865; he has permission to hold and occupy the said
tract, subject to such regulations as may be established by
proper authority; and all persons are prohibited from interfer-
ing with *him* or *his* possession of the same.

By command of
R. Saxton

Brev't Maj. General

A. P. Ketchum Lt A[ide] D[e] C[amp][15]

Wilson's Hanging Bull tract of forty acres was carved
from land he may have worked at fourteen, before the
war—if he was the most likely of the four Wilson boys
born on Sapelo in the 1830s and 1840s. Hanging Bull had
been the plantation of Catherine Spalding Kenan and her
husband, Michael J. Kenan, and its adjacent hammock
was home to the descendants of Bilali's three daughters,
Minto, Margaret, and Hester, who had been the Kenans'
slaves.[16] It was not just getting land, but getting back to
that home that led Cotto Grovner, Margaret's daughter,
to go into an army office in Savannah and ask permission
to go back to Sapelo: "March was comin' and time to

plant."[17] The request granted, she, her husband, John Grovner, and their four children, as they had done to reach Savannah, walked the fifty miles to the mainland across from the island. Decades later a girl in the family, Katie Brown, could still remember how sore their feet got; in the evenings, Cotto would heat water to bathe them. And they made it home.

For other refugees, Sapelo was an unknown quanitity. Destitute people who had never seen a barrier island were sent to the half-dozen biggest islands stretching south as far as Florida. Such a person would arrive with a sixty-day "Colored Pass" to join those already on the islands raising food crops. One such person was Wallace Macintosh (whose name suggests that he may have been from McIntosh County, if not Sapelo):

May 24, 1865

Permission is hereby granted to
Wallace Macintosh
with your effects
to *Sapelo—"Chocolate Plantation" R. Spalding's*
to settle and return within 60 days.[18]

R. Saxton   A. P. Ketchum

The islands had become displaced persons' camps and were precariously supporting larger populations than they had in slave days. On June 16, Campbell reported proudly that he had settled 317 people on St. Catherines and 214 adults and 98 children on Sapelo, which, by July, reportedly had nine hundred settlers.[19] It is not clear how those returning got along with the newcomers, but, as we will see, they were not to be neighbors for long.

A sizable number of those nine hundred were returning Sapelo people, and they and some other settlers were to be permanent farmers on the island. And now Saxton had important new authorization for his program of land distribution. In March 1865, Congress passed—and President Lincoln signed—an act creating the Bureau of Refugees, Freedmen and Abandoned Lands. Saxton was made assistant commissioner for South Carolina and Georgia, and he and his staff took seriously the legislation's Section 4: "*And be it further enacted,* That the Commissioner, under the direction of the President, shall have the authority to set apart, for the use of loyal refugees and freedmen, such tracts of land within the insurrectionary States as shall have been abandoned . . . and to every male citizen, whether refugee or freedman . . . there shall be assigned not more than forty acres of such land." The land was to be rented for three years, after which "the occupants may purchase the land and receive such title thereto as the United States can convey. . . ."[20]

For refugees who had come back to a familiar island, Sherman's stern order and Congress's matter-of-fact call for distribution of abandoned lands in plots of "forty acres" reflected the basic logic that Robert Frost was to grasp in "The Gift Outright": "The land was ours before we were the land's."[21] There was, the poet recognized, a fundamental change in the relationship of people to a place they inhabit that comes about long after the first grasp of the invader on a stretch of geography. It has little to do with something called personal property or real estate law. In time—it may not even take long—that land comes to possess us, to give us grounding, to allow us to know who we are, where we belong. It doesn't in the end even have to be topographically distinguished; we gain something of our identity, our sense of being a part of the whole, from some almost innate loyalty to whatever is a space called home.

For some of us that space, not protected by Doboy Sound, is hard to define. For the people of Sapelo it hasn't been hard at all. In a cruel reworking of Frost's sense of his own forebears' first hold on the land, the Sapelo people first came onto their island as possessions themselves— they were the Spaldings' before they were the island's, but they shifted the possessive. Places have a way of defying being property; ownership, in fact, is not as secure a concept as owners think. The Spaldings may have thought they owned those thousand human beings whom they called their people—they had legal title to them—but they were wrong. By working the island's land, by laughing, weeping, praying on it, being born and dying on it, the former slaves traded possessors and became the island's, and it became theirs.

As a fundamental result of the revolution that the Civil War was, these people were no longer legally owned. And yet, in a curious, benign way they still were. The island itself had, long ago, taken them in, given them raw comfort, demanded rigorous loyalty—had made them Sapelo's people.

Sherman's order and federal law made the relationship reciprocal. Sapelo's people were going back—being drawn back—to where they belonged. They were spared the camps of refugees that had been established on portions of the Spalding lands and took possession of their hammocks. Now their places in Shell Hammock, in Belle Marsh, in

Hanging Bull would belong to them. These settlements—the hammocks on Sapelo—although desperately in need of reclaiming from neglect, did not need establishing. They were already in place, waiting for the homecomers to rejoin those they had been forced to leave behind, their relatives who had lived out the war on the island.

But it was not, as Fergus Wilson discovered, simply their old patches of land in the hammock which were to be theirs. The lands abandoned by the Spalding family were to be divided and freed people settled on them. Sampson Hogg, Bilally Smith, Liberty Bell would amply meet Sherman's requirement that whenever "three respectable negroes, heads of families, shall desire to settle on land, and shall have selected for that purpose an island or a locality clearly defined within the limits . . . the Inspector of Settlements and Plantations will . . . give them a license to settle."[22]

A good many Sapelo people were still stranded in Savannah, along with thousands of inland people who had fled to the coast. And yet, stranded is not the right word. A person, if still alive, can, unlike a beached whale, be helped up from the dry, destitute shore of war. Contrary to common belief, there is no contradiction between independence and accepting assistance. Solitary we are not. For refugees to whom the coast was alien territory, the situation was desperate. They did not know where they could come to rest and were being sent to Sapelo and other islands. The islanders, on the other hand, were anxious to go home, and, for them, help came from one of the most remarkable men ever to enter the Sapelo story, Tunis Campbell.

Campbell, the son of a free black blacksmith in Middlebrook, New Jersey, began his education in 1817 with the help of a white friend of the family, in an Episcopal school in Babylon, New York. Later, he became a steward and waiter in hotels in New York City and Boston and wrote *Hotel Keepers, Head Waiters, and Housekeepers' Guide,* a manual for the staffs of hotels.

As early as 1849, he was one of seven speakers, along with Frederick Douglass, at a rally of African Americans opposing colonization, the plan for the exporting of them to Africa or the Caribbean. In 1853, Campbell was an official at the Colored National Convention held in Rochester, New York—learning the art of politics. Then, at age fifty, the war gave him the opportunity to put the skill to practice. In 1863, after joining efforts to persuade President Lincoln and Secretary of War Stanton that black people should be employed in the work of assisting newly freed Southerners, he was finally accepted for service under General Saxton. Campbell, like other African Americans eager to help, but ignorant of the South, sought, as he put it, "to instruct and elevate the colored race."[23]

Arriving mustached and in a city suit in Beaufort on Port Royal Island in 1863, Campbell, lean and precise, like Charlotte Forten and other educated, urban African-American members of Gideon's Band, had a lot of learning to do before he could even understand the people he sought to "elevate." Campbell learned quickly, and in April 1865 Saxton appointed him a civilian agent of the Freedmen's Bureau in Savannah, with instructions to take charge of the Georgia sea islands.

Some sense not only of the anguish of the refugees, but also of Campbell's realistic attention to their needs is suggested by the fate of a group of freed people trying to get to St. Catherines Island, north of Sapelo. The *Enoch Dean*, crammed with people on their way with all their possessions from Savannah to the island, capsized and sank. The *Savannah Daily Herald* reported that all the passengers and the crew survived, but lost were most of the refugees' few possessions and, critically, seed and farming equipment that Campbell had provided.

The *Enoch Dean* was but one of many ships that carried freed families out to the island. In April, coming down from Beaufort, Campbell's boat stopped "and Savannah loaded us as deep as we could swim" with people, their rations, and some seed to plant. It was to be feed-yourself welfare. "As the season is late, I have begun to work on Sapolow Island, Georgia," he wrote the National Freedman's Relief Association in New York. "I want you to get me ten barrels of sweet potatoes, seed [potatoes] . . ." and the old restaurant man told the New Yorkers exactly where on John Street or Water Street they could be bought. [24]

It is difficult to know what the relationships were between the refugees for whom the islands were a new place and the returning Sapelo families. And difficult as well to be sure just how intact were the family units of the people returning. No doubt some family members did not make it back; it is equally likely that some of those who did brought new partners. Of the sixty-two family units identified (with surnames) in the 1870 census—by then, as we shall see, the other refugees had left—only twelve cannot be verified as having a prewar connection to Sapelo, and there is every reason to think that some of these, if not all, did. A comparison of given names in the twelve families as listed in the census to those recorded as Spalding slaves (surnames not given) reinforces the contention that virtually all of the postwar Sapelo people had lived on the island earlier or were married to those who had.

They had come home. Home to find relatives who had never left and others, like Sampson Hogg, who had found their own way back—back to familiar fields. Three years is long enough for weeds to fill and brush to invade once carefully cultivated acreage. There was work to do if a late spring crop was to be gotten in. There was no one to order them to plant; now the discipline to get up and to cut and clear, to plow and hoe, had to come from themselves. They were on their own.

7

Hanging Bull

In March 1859, Pierce Butler sold four hundred people. The *New York Tribune* carried a long, thorough description of the sale of longtime inhabitants of Butler's Island and of another of Butler's plantations, on the northern tip of St. Simons Island, immediately to the south of Sapelo. Taken to Savannah, roughly $400,000 worth of an indebted Butler's assets were "consigned to the care of Mr. J. Bryan, Auctioneer and Negro Broker, who was to feed and keep them in condition until disposed of. Immediately on their arrival they were taken to the Race Course, and there quartered in the sheds erected for the accommodation of the horses and carriages of the gentlemen attending the races."

The account is detailed and graphic; the story of Jeffrey, "chattel No. 319," and of Dorcas, "chattel No. 278," is not untypical. They were auctioned: "In another hour," noted the reporter, "I see Dorcas in the long room, sitting motionless as a statue. . . . And I see Jeffrey, who goes to his new master, pulls off his hat and says, 'I'se very much obliged, mas'r, to you for trying to help me [by buying my wife] . . . thank you—but—it's—berry—hard'—and here the poor fellow breaks down entirely and walks away covering his face with his battered hat, and sobbing like a child.

"He is soon surrounded by a group of his colored friends, who, with an instinctive delicacy . . . stand quiet . . . about him."[1]

Less than a decade—but fully a revolution—later the Sapelo neighbors of these sold chattels, once equally vulnerable, were living in a different world. In 1865, they had a school; in 1866, a church; in 1867 the men voted—and all lived together in secure families.

The Hammocks

Energy is not the word that leaps at you in Hog Hammock today; it is exactly the right word for life on the island in 1865. It perfectly describes the response of Sapelo's people to that other elusive word, freedom. They had come home to make a new life out of a place old with memory.

There was no need for Tunis Campbell, busy governing his new domain, to tell these freed people how or where to settle. They simply went back to the hammocks in which they had lived before the war. Minto Bell and her sister Hester Smith, both in their nineties (and very likely among the other "superannuated" people the Union Navy doctor had met on his exploring expedition) were rejoined at Hanging Bull, on the island's west side, by Hester's son Bilally Smith; his wife, Hagar; and Minto's sons, Liberty, Bilally, Abram, and Fortune Bell, and their families.

A younger generation settled in as well. Allen Smith, he who had "walked from Macon," married his second cousin Phoebe Bell "about 1865." They probably started their family in Hanging Bluff; later they moved to Raccoon Bluff. There, high over the inlet on the island's northeast shoulder, they joined Baileys, Walkers, and Grovners, as well as Sampson Hogg and his wife, Sally Smith (another of Hester Smith's daughters), and their six children, ranging in age from nine to fifteen. Later the Hoggs moved to the center of the island and founded Hog Hammock.

There were Greens and Hillerys at Chocolate, the deliciously rendered name of a place on the western side of the island owned in the eighteenth century by a royalist Frenchman—the Carters and Greens were at nearby Burbon, pronounced on the island "Bur Boon." Joneses were at Belle Marsh; others were at Drink Water and in a cluster of cabins at Shell Hammock, on a spit of land just south of the big, neglected house that the Spaldings had left behind.

The essential job was to get food crops in the ground. The plots that had been worked during the war to grow vegetables for the Union sailors would still have been in good condition. On the other hand, the hundreds of cotton acres were rank and barren. The islanders had long depended on their house plots, the acre or two around each cabin, for food—it is not clear whether, once these plots were tilled, the Spaldings supplied rations or required their slaves to feed themselves. It would appear that the slaves were expected to be self-sufficient—to care for their own "chickens and hogs and even cattle and sometimes a horse"; a slave could also "cultivate small patches of ground where he would raise vegetables."[2]

March and Fannie Carter, in their early forties, had to clear their house plot and feed it with seaweed to bring the resilient sea island soil back into production. Their four children were only beginning to be able to help around the place; the oldest, the twins, Phoebe and Glasco, were only eleven. As the Carters and their neighbors knew, reclamation was tough work; the difference was that it was work done on one's own account. There was a future that was not someone else's.

The School

In the beginning there was the school. Tunis Campbell knew how much the one he had attended in New York had meant to him. He knew too that only with the power of the word could any other power be within the freedmen's grasp. On Sapelo, the patriarch Bilali had clung to that knowledge through the whole of his long life. Mentally shackled to a manual-labor servitude that prevented the growth of his scholarly learning, he clung to his tiny fragment of writing—his own writing. Literacy mattered if one were to best know Allah, know God, if one were to confront the threatening complexities of the secular world.

Now, in June 1865—two months after the war and a century since one of the family had been in school—Bilali's great- and great-great-grandchildren were studying in a classroom, as was Liberty Bell, his adult grandson.

Campbell reported at the end of the month that sixty students were enrolled. More wanted to be: "We cannot take anymore [students] at present as we have not got books for them. There are a great many adults who want to go also but we cannot take them," he reported in a plea for more educational materials later that summer.[3]

The next year, Campbell informed the American Missionary Association (supported largely by members of New England Congregational churches) that there was need for three more schools on Sapelo. It appears from the sparse remaining records that his call was heeded to the tune of at least one other school. By 1870, one Anthony Wilson was the teacher of the Sun Shine School, so named lest his students be left "in their blindness." He reported that he had twenty-three scholars in his Sun Shine School on "Sapelo Isle," twelve male, eleven female. Nineteen were "always Present, nineteen "always Punctual"; twenty were paying tuition, amount unstated. It is interesting that the school was racially integrated; four of the children of Thomas and Jane Heson (he was a ship's carpenter) were in school.[4]

Of Wilson's other pupils, four were over sixteen and, without elaboration, Wilson noted that seven were in "Night School." It is not clear whether these seven, presumably adults, were in addition to the four or included them. What *is* suggested is that he and his Northern sponsors regarded adult education as important to the creation of a responsible citizenry. In all, Wilson had managed to turn eight students into readers during the past year. In addition to making this slow progress, he reported teaching twenty-five members of the Sun Shine Sabbath School.

The 1870 census taker listed sixty pupils among the

"inhabitants of Sapelo Island."[5] (He did not indicate where on the island people lived or the locale of the schools.) Of the sixty, fourteen were nineteen years old or older. The children began school at about six; the youngest pupil was Mary Heson, the white ship's carpenter's daughter. Liberty and Diannah Bell, forty-eight and thirty-seven years old, were the only husband-and-wife students. Their thirteen-year-old son was not in school, but Rose Gardner attended with three of her children. Nannie Lemon, the mother of a deaf-and-dumb girl and of three infants as well, was in school.[6]

Despite the example of these scholars, there was not a consistent pattern of education on the island. Indeed, most of the adults—indentified as, for example, "Farmer" or "Keeping House"—and teenagers—listed as "Works on farm" or "at home"—were in the census taker's "cannot read" and "cannot write" columns. Forty-one children, including the Lemon child who was "deaf and dumb," were not in school. Only four of the fifty-nine families were headed by men who were fully literate, but sixty pupils, accounting for nearly a fifth of the total island population of 334 (a number which included a good many infants and the white neighbors), were in school. There were no completely literate families and not sufficient totally illiterate ones to suggest a hierarchical structure based on learning in the communities, and there was parity in terms of males and females among the younger pupils.

All the members of Fortune and Phoebe Bell's extended family who were over six were in class, as were all of Abram and Nancy Bell's children. Although neither Sampson nor Sally Hogg could read or write, all save one of their children were in school, including seventeen-year-old Shadrack—Shad Hall. Glasco and George Handy ("day laborers 28 and 26"), Peter Maxwell, a thirty-seven-year-old farmer who had fought with the 33rd U.S. Colored Volunteers, James Walker, twenty-six and also a farmer, Bermuda Lemon, who worked on his father's farm, and John Lemon, another forty-eight-year-old scholar, either shared the room with children decades younger than they or attended in the evening. Sapelo's early scholars were a diverse—and eager—lot.

There are post–Civil War photographs of dedicated schoolmarms from the North, white, surrounded by enthralled children, black, that accurately pay tribute to both teachers and students. But such would have been out of focus on Sapelo, as a skirmish over teachers—both male—makes clear. On March 28, 1870, Charley Lemon, Fortune Bell, Bilally Smith, Allen Smith, Liberty Bell, Sampson Hogg, and five other Sapelo men—all adults—wrote to the American Missionary Association complaining of their teacher, Anthony Wilson: "he would not teach Regular as he ought to do."[7] The Freedmen complained that though they had paid him, he had left the island—Wilson had been the teacher on Sapelo at least since 1869—and on returning was not teaching as they wanted him to. All of the signers did so with an X, and the letter bore the additional signature of "Charly Marshall." Charles H. Marshall was not a disinterested party; he hoped to succeed Wilson as teacher.

In May, a counterargument was mounted in a letter to the AMA signed simply "Sun Shine School." As a teacher, Anthony Wilson had reason to be proud of the author of the letter's stilted, but communicative, command of language; indeed, he may have been proud of himself. The handwriting appears to be identical to that of Wilson's report to the AMA of January.

Why, the writer wondered, had the AMA sent Charles Marshall to replace Wilson? Wilson "have always taught us to read the precious Bible . . . we are perfectly satisfied with him here he have taught our Children from addition up to long division [;] we have had several teachers before him but he knows more [than they.]" The letter specifically refers to the fact that Wilson taught not only the children but also adults and refers to the teacher as "brother A. Wilson," which underscores the likelihood that Wilson, like his students and Marshall, was a black man.[8] This is highly probable, as the American Missionary Association sent almost no white male teachers south.

"We refuse to give up our Teacher Anthony Wilson. . . . [He] work Cheaper than any teacher we have had. . . . We do not want Charles Marshall," the writer insisted. And he or she had a point; Charles Marshall's later letters to the AMA's General Field Agent, the Reverend Edward P. Smith in New York, giving his side of the argument, are virtually illiterate. He cannot even manage his signature, "Charly Marshall," without crossing out his first try at "Charly."[9]

In New York, Smith proposed to solve the problem with not one but two white Northern female teachers, which may not have sat well with the determined black students on the island. He enlisted Tunis Campbell in an effort to resolve the school crisis on the island. Campbell, now the leading politician in Sapelo's McIntosh County, recognized that his constituents on the island cared deeply about their school. In August he had an ally, Simms

North, write (on his senatorial stationery) to Smith: "I think Misses Russell & Champney will succeed in reviving a prosperous school [on Sapelo]. But it will be a hard job, and Miss R. does not want to try it and will not unless you will back them." The two needed to have their transportation paid for and their board on the island assured.[10] He thought it likely that the Peabody Fund, a philanthropy sponsoring schools in the South, might well provide the funds.

Broadening his subject, North reported confidently to Smith that the Georgia legislature was "working up an excellent school bill and I *think it will go through within two weeks*. . . . This work must be *kept moving*."[11] North and Campbell's unyielding optimism had led to an over-evaluation; as one student of public education in Georgia concludes, the "law of 1870 provided for a State Board of Education but the board lacked the authority to accomplish its mission."[12] The act called for apportionment of funds based on the number of students and envisioned the establishment of schools for all children, although "with instruction of white and colored Youth in separate schools."[13]

Rufus Bullock, the progressive Republican governor, sought to strengthen the schools by appointing a Pennsylvanian and former Freedmen's Bureau official to be the first commissioner of education. But when Bullock left the governorship and black legislators like Campbell lost power, the attention to thorough education of the black students was left in the hands of local authorities, which, as in McIntosh County, meant white people made the choices of teachers.[14] There was not even a cure to Marshall's problem: "the law of 1870 stated no educational background was necessary for teachers to be employed."[15]

It is not clear how the Wilson–Marshall feud was resolved, but what that quarrel does reveal is the intense interest the freedpeople took in their schools. That concern heightened the enormous frustration they, semiliterate at best, must have felt trying, at great distance from the administrator of their school, to have some say in who would teach them—and, we can guess, what they were to be taught. The struggle over the control as well as the nature of the education of the freedpeople was not simply between white Northern missionaries and white Georgians; the students themselves were deeply involved.[16]

Daily records of the American Missionary schools on Sapelo do not survive, and it is difficult to know how lasting had been the initial undertaking to train adults so that they could gain the small, but essential, grasp on power that learning would have given them. The zeal on the part of the Northern reformers to assist the freedpeople, strong at the war's end, receded rapidly. Up on St. Helena Island in South Carolina, Laura Towne, from Philadelphia, continued her school at what is still called the Penn Center, and over fifty of the "predominantly Negro" colleges across the South, crucial in the black community ever since, were opened. Eleven Northern women teachers in Georgia withstood the animosity of white supremacists and a degree of resentment from their black students and held fast to their schools for twenty years following the war, but to a large extent, the reformers yielded to what was touted as a progressive public school plan.

Sapelo's school did not close. In 1878, there were 139 children in Sapelo's school and it was still integrated; Mary

Heson and four of her siblings attended. The school was no longer a private missionary school, but had been incorporated into the county public school system. Progress has its price. Things were made orderly; classes were scheduled only in the daytime. Now none of the pupils was older than sixteen; education was for girls and boys. Adult illiteracy had not been overcome and the dangerous business of educating adults, men and women, for citizenship had been closed down.

Four years later, in 1882, many of those in school were children of earlier students; Sipio Bell, a teenager in school just after the war, now had two of his own children, Margaret and Thomas, enrolled. And generation after generation, schooling continued on the island, but it produced neither the power of the word nor the mastery of their world that the freedpeople of 1865 had sought so eagerly.

If schooling had been the beginning for the Sapelo people, with both children and adults enrolled, the hope that education would provide the great leap forward was recognized as illusory early on. As early as 1869, on the mainland, an American Missionary Association teacher reported proudly that her students were doing three-figure multiplication, but their handicap was not the three miles they were walking each day to reach school. It was the bleak future that lay before them. Their parents "are generally very poor. They work mostly on rice plantations and are paid in orders on stores in which their employers are usually interested. They see little if any money—many think themselves fortunate if they do not come out in debt to the establishment."[17] Sharecropping and the lien system—liens on the value of crops to pay for the things needed to raise them—did not take hold on Sapelo, as we will see, but there as elsewhere in McIntosh County— in the South—poverty closed down on the promise that education had once held out.

There is no school on Sapelo now. * There still was when Matty Carter's son Jake was a grammar-school pupil shortly after World War II. His teacher there, "Mr. Nobles," urged Jake to go for further schooling to Darien, where he attended the Todd Grant School—named for a "free man of color" who, during Reconstruction, had been successful in the lumber business. There Jake found his old teacher was now teaching.

The Todd Grant 1957 yearbook is like all high school yearbooks, sugared in sentiment—Vivian Ann Spaulding says she'll have a golden chair waiting in heaven for Jake— but it's a reminder of other matters as well. 1957 was three years after the *Brown v. Board of Education* Supreme Court decision declaring segregated schools to be uncon- stitutional, and light-years before integration came to remote McIntosh County.

There is in Jake's yearbook not only a reminder of that great decision's fundamental correctness, but also a tinge of a certain loss that accompanied it. There is a picture of only one white person in the book, the superintendent of the school system, and the words she commended to the students' memory suggests precisely why *Brown* was right.

* The present local superintendent of schools in Darien is contemplating an interesting experiment. She proposes boating mainland students to the is- land, reopening the schoolhouse, and, with the assistance of the University of Georgia's Marine Institute, teaching marine biology.

She wishes the students well in their "further training" and "employment"—there is no hint that a door to college even exists.

But the message conveyed by the formal, dignified portraits of the faculty—Mr. James B. Nobles among them—is that there was strength in that school. It's impossible from the yearbook to know anything much of the content of classroom assignments and discussions, but the inscriptions from the other students to Jake give us a hint of the powerful text in the margins of the classroom work. One after another, the students remind him that they must look to the future; must not be held back by the past.

Chester Arthur DeVillars wears the heartiest of smiles in his principal's photograph. It's best not to guess how great a price in deference to Sheriff Tom Poppell, who controlled whites-only McIntosh County, that smile disguised. Mr. DeVillars, in his inscription, privately defying, as so many black teachers did, his superintendent, urged Jake to go on to college, which then would have meant Savannah State or Fort Valley. Instead, Jake went that other route that has carried so many black high school graduates forward—entrance into the army. (That propulsion has carried *their* children still farther forward; it is astonishing how large is the percentage of black college graduates in America today who are from service families.)

Jake Carter went into the army as a private. Thirty years and seventeen days later he came out a major. Sapelo is not a place to put you in mind of war. But war has its way of working its own mind. I was reminded of this when I met Jake and learned that he had served three tours of duty in Vietnam; I had already known that there is no corner of the country into which war does not intrude when I spotted emblems of another conflict, the yellow ribbons of the Gulf War—only one or two, but there they were pinned onto pine trees in Hog Hammock.

Jake did not come home to Sapelo to live when he retired; he comes now from North Carolina to visit his mother—his well-groomed poodle, Patches, bounces around Matty Carter's neater-than-ever garden; she, in jeans, sweater, and head rag, is in fine form. She's as proud of this Jake as she is held to the memory of his father, her other Jake. And while he's home, Jake has gone for a run on Sapelo's great, flat beach.

Doing so, he might have encountered another runner. James Banks, Jr., is a senior at Georgia Southern University in Statesboro. At twenty-two, he's deep-chested and strong—poised and friendly with a nice dash of dignity, but, somehow, it's not hard imagining him at age six on the seven-o'clock boat and on his way to first grade.

Progress had played its usual game of lurching along behind its initial promise. When Georgia got around to reintegrating its schools, all of Sapelo's children began attending school, from the earliest grades, on the mainland. In the winter now, in the dark, the seven-o'clock boat makes a roomy school bus for the Alfred Bailey children, Cornelia Bailey's foster-care children, Argene Grovner's and the few other island children; it's not a crowded bus, but a wonderfully restless one. And at the Meridian dock there is, in fact, a bus to carry them the last ten miles into school in Darien. (They turn around and come back on the three-thirty boat.)

James's first three years of school were in Eulonia, a community just north of Meridian, where the pupils were about evenly divided racially. For grades four through seven, he went to Darien for classes, roughly 55 percent black, 45 percent white; these were held in the old Todd Grant. The proud old black high school had been demoted. Todd Grant, a "pretty good" school then, "better now"—as James recalls it—readied Banks for high school, the (public) McIntosh County Academy.

There he and another islander, Leonard Walker, played on the basketball team. To stretch their young bodies, the two, out on Sapelo, would ride their bicycles to the South Beach, down the sand road grassed over as it breaks from the woods just east of Hog Hammock, where they lived. If the weather was warm, they would be in swimming trunks—and into the mild surf; more often Leonard and James would run together on the wide, flat, hard beach. And James remembers running alone. He recalls the beach's beauty, which he took for granted, but remembers, too, the loneliness of those runs. It would have been more fun running with a friend, he says. But friends close to his age on the island were few; Leonard was the only person from Hog Hammock in his class.

Loyalty to the island is strongly a part of James Banks, but for a long time he knew that one day he would have to leave. The obvious route ahead for an ambitious young black man was the service. It was more or less assumed that one branch or another of the armed forces would be, for him as for so many African Americans, a way out of the dead end of a neighborhood. But Banks got slanted in a different direction—by his basketball coach and mathematics teacher. When Cleveland Butler from Camden County, south of Darien, heard that his hard-driving forward was headed for the Air Force, he said, wait a minute, there are other choices. Of course, I wouldn't try to talk you out of going into the service—but he did.

There were also, I suspect, some subterranean messages

coming from James's parents. When he talked of the Air Force at home, his quiet and quietly determined mother, as he remembers it, said, "It's your life," and made it clear that she would support him in whatever choice he might make. And her strategy worked; everything I hear about Matty and James Banks, Sr.—and you hear the best of things—suggests that they had more in mind for their children than any path of least resistance. If (rarely) parents are truly skillful, their children are the last to know some steering is going on. The direction that the Bankses and Coach Butler had in mind was college.

Their daughter, Shannon, more shy than her brother, but no less determined and serious, is a student at Georgia Southern too. James, two years older, like his sister, is doing well. Darien Academy prepared him for college satisfactorily in mathematics, but he needed help with his writing. When he gets his bachelor's degree in this summer's quarter, he will start graduate work. Banks doesn't know yet just where that will lead him. He knows of good work done in a drug treatment program for men his age in Brunswick; he thinks too of being a counselor in a high school and encouraging others as his coach did him. James Banks, Jr., is on his appointed way.

For this one islander, the Jeffersonian dream that education could be the "guarantor of freedom" seems to be working. James is free of limits which the tiny island community imposes and which no amount of sentiment can hide, but he is empowered by values that family and community have instilled in him. James, his sister Shannon, another university student, Melissa Walker—and, back over time, Elizabeth Elaine Lemon, the embodiment, in his own day, of John Dewey's faith in education as the maker of the true citizen—are among the few islanders for whom education has done so powerful a job.

But for most, the flash of faith in 1865, at the close of a terrible war, that, somehow, schooling—achieving the word—would carry a whole people forward into a freedom that had true meaning lost its fire. Or that fire was allowed to be lost by a society afraid of what might happen if it risked the creation of an educated citizenry—a citizenry that included once-slaves come home to Sapelo.

8

First African Baptist Church

If the schoolhouse was not enough of a structure to carry the weight of a whole new world, perhaps a churchhouse would be. In May 1866, Sapelo's people gathered to found the First Baptist Church. They raised their first building on the bank of Hanging Bull Creek in the hammock where Minto Bell and her sons lived.[1] There, on that first day, to bring the church into being were the founders, Abram and Bilally Bell, two of Minto's sons, two of Bilali's grandsons.

That building, on the island's west side, was destroyed in the great hurricane of 1898. The church's second home was built in Raccoon Bluff of fine, durable lumber from another building blown apart by that storm. (Its second name was the First African Baptist Church.) Allen Green took me to the church, his church, the day we rode on the neglected road to Raccoon Bluff. With windows closed, as brush raked the sides of his truck, we passed clearings where his house had been and where relatives' houses had been. And then, to the left, was the lonely command of the stern weather-worn church, elegant and as starkly simple as a Protestant chapel on a Swiss hillside.

The structure, its dimensions true, is a generous rectangle topped with a peaked roof and bell tower. A rightly proportioned vestibule projects from one end, the small deacon's room for the preacher and deacons to ready themselves at the other. Once, before the roof was lowered, there was a gallery and two hundred people worshiped here. Every first Sunday, a preacher, from Ludovici, a mainland town well in from the coast, came on Saturday, ate, spent the night with a parishioner, preached, ate again, preached again—and left. On other Sundays, one of Sapelo's own deacons led the long service, to which people from all over the island would walk five, six, seven miles.

This deep commitment to Christianity was manifested in a church founded by grandsons of a devout Muslim. That religious about-face would appear to support the contention that Christianity totally obliterated all forms of African religious practices among African-Americans. Some church scholars argue that this happened; they haven't been inside a Southern black Baptist church.

There is no echo of Africa in the building. None until you go inside and imagine people filling the emptiness in the lovely light coming through the windows. The deacons entering in procession from their room to the side of the preacher's platform would have been as formal and correct as London bankers, but they were coming into a room eager with gathering parishioners ready to swell into life. And that life is one of a religion that is physical in its reality. The self, the body, is not silenced or constrained, not separate from some piously transfigured spirit. There is no dark hush. People have come to join hands, to participate. From the first antiphonal responses to a deacon's welcome, with voices swelling with the opening hymn, all is communal. What would formally be termed congregational responses—the progressively more vocal interruptions of the preacher's prayers and sermon—are, instead, the message itself. These people are in conversation with a lord who is a member of the family.

Here there is no proper upper-middle-class white American Protestant reverential silence. Neither is there the vulgarity of the sneakers-and-shorts casualness of an evangelical temple. Instead, there is energetic seriousness. On Sapelo there is not the elegant, stylized movement of the famous McIntosh County Shout, the ceremony of religious dance practiced just down the road from Meridian a few miles away, but in the rising and moving about the church there is a physical lunge into a faith that sustains.

And, in candor, which obfuscates. The message of the pulpit is not a message; it is an incantation which demands of the congregation a fervent response. The minister neither provides a theological exegesis nor pays attention to the secular problems of a community in which he is only a monthly visitor. The illumination comes instead from the communicants, who know that they are there precisely because they must be. There is in the room the unmistakable evidence of election; there is no doubting Thomas in their house.

The house of worship now is not the empty building in abandoned Raccoon Bluff, but a simple, carefully painted—a bright white—stucco-on-cinderblock struc-

ture, fronted with neatly trimmed shrubs, at the north end
of Hog Hammock. It is there, on this first Sunday in May
1991, 125 years after angels of their better nature gathered
and made joyful noise, Sapelo's people, slowly, sedately,
but rich in anticipation, come together outside today's
First African Baptist Church.

Climbing down from vans and pickup trucks, the men
stand at the edge of the shade in black suits; the women
moving into the shelter of the large oak wear hats plastic
and giddy, straw and smart. You have read wrong if you
interpret this exquisite, conscious attention to dress as def-
erential respect for someone else's sense of correctness.
From head to patent-leather toe, these people are, this
day, adorned for celebration. They have come to make
the Lord's day a fine party.

Caution is in order when you come upon this postcard-
perfect embodiment of the American picturesque. Ladies,
straight-backed in good, soft, dark silk and wide-brimmed
hats, are sitting not as if posed, but rather as they are,
perfectly at ease on an unpainted plank bench abutting a
giant live oak, its leaves filtering the light of a warming
morning. It will be a long morning, but there is not a
whisper of impatience. This Sunday morning is moving
as Sunday mornings have moved here for 125 proud, con-
fident years.

The vans, pickups, and William Banks, Jr.'s, massive
funereal battleship-gray ex-schoolbus, labeled "First African Baptist Church" and scrubbed within an inch of its
lumbering life, keep going to Marsh Landing and coming
back with relatives arriving from Miami, New York, and
the whole out-of-step stretch between. (It isn't easy to
maintain your dignity and your hat sitting up in the back

of a pickup, but here it's an art mastered.) By now, there are, perhaps, two hundred of us in the churchyard.

Sunday school over, we move inside for the anniversary service. I slide into a rear pew far over on the men's left side of the congregation. One off-island white friend is sitting with me; two white women from the south end are over with the ladies; and I find myself, in a rash of something akin to thinking politics, celebrity department—a slippage that rarely afflicts you on the island—curious about earlier visitors to the First ABC. President Jimmy Carter, Rosalynn Carter, and Amy Carter were here on Easter Sunday in 1979. Those estimable Georgians—and ardent Baptists—would have been more at home than this nonbeliever, although I did find Bible stories and, particularly, hymns out of a Protestant childhood flooding back conveniently as the long service worked its energy through the morning.

What had been on the president's mind as he let himself into this congregation's absorption of religion? How banished were whatever pileup of lethal international mishaps that had inevitably trailed him to Sapelo? And how fundamentally like and different from his church in Plains was the African-American church here on the coast? On one level, he must have felt a touch of chagrin. To his dismay, his southwest Georgian congregation in Plains had refused admission to black Baptists who, one morning, had sought to join them. There had been no such rebuff here.

On Sapelo there is a nice nonchalance, balanced in equal measure with deeply respectful pride, in the memory of the presidential visit. Viola Johnson's store, given over now largely to her grapevine-basket-making, is rung round with pictures of the Carters—eating her late husband's famous barbecue and smiling into cameras; there were a good many rolls of film shot that Easter weekend. But, to a nice degree, Carter—and I—are put in our place by a hint that he was just another white boy over to take a look.

Speculations like these yield to the insistence of the service itself. "Silent Night," blissfully out of season, never rocked and rolled as cheerfully before. As happens every time I hear it, "Amazing Grace" took me back to my son's high school graduation when his class president skipped the seemingly obligatory speech and, simply, unaccompanied and alone, sang the wonderful workhorse. Some clichés bear hanging onto.

I concentrated on the sermon, determined not to be dismissive out of either ignorance or snobbery. The slightly dotty old pastor began tentatively, even seemed confused. And then he warmed to his task and I realized that there were almost no complete sentences and that what passed for one bore no connection to that before or following. It was an antiphonal litany; it might have been in Latin, if one could have been sure that the parishioners had heard the same Latin all their lives. Snatches of Biblical phrases, pieces of Christian dogma, each with just enough of the signaling code, brought forth the demanded or, rather, confidently expected "yes" and "amen" responses.

This for well over an hour, until it dissolved into a chant and, perhaps, the closing hymn, by which time I no longer trusted that there would ever be an ending. Not alone, I found myself excusing my way out of the pew. As I made my escape from the intruding, incongruous, unstoppable preacher and burst into the church's little vestibule, I rushed past my pew mate, Jack Leigh, and Glasco

Bailey sitting on two sedate chairs having a quietly civilized conversation. They, better than I, had known when enough was enough.

Later, outside, under the live oak, waiting for the promised feast, Bailey stands tall, somehow a head taller than he had been bent over the turkeys. His brown worsted suit fits his big frame; he is erect as he stands with two athletic twenty-year-olds back for the day and as bright-eyed and handsome as Glasco Bailey was—and is.

Decades of teaching nineteen-year-olds have made me shameless, and I walk right over. Leonard Walker is the son of Tracy Walker, the captain of the *Sapelo Queen*, with the lithe reach of a basketball player—this is James Banks's teammate—but one not tall enough to capitalize on the fact. Introducing myself, I learn that he's studying criminology at a south Georgia college and, in my mind, immediately peg him for a good future—maybe a lawyer. This could make sense in a family that's been through a terrible trouble with crime.

Turning to Glasco's other friend, I realize that I had spotted him sitting several rows in front of me in church—his back spreading to burst a loud olive-green shirt. In the tightly packed pews and outside, now, under the trees, in a sea of somber dark male suits, he stands out. The shirt is a small act of defiance that he has the presence, even the charisma, to carry off. Talking to him, I find that he works out in a gym in Brunswick, near his job. No college—yet—but, somehow, I sense good things ahead for him too. His name is Kendall, or something like it—and, it turns out, he is a cousin of James.

In the bright May light, Sapelo's hold on its churches is past doubt, but not even as euphoric a moment as this celebration of 125 years of religious freedom erased the never-forgettable fact that these people, remote on their island, are, nonetheless, colored people in a land of careless hatred. There had been a time when there seemed a chance that hatred could be downed. A year after they founded their church, the people of Sapelo's hammocks had taken great care to achieve in the secular realm that purchase on freedom that they had mastered in the spiritual.

In 1867, their forebears walked through another open door. The United States Congress, dismayed by the systematic efforts to suppress the recently freed people in the South, sought to ensure their safety (and passed along to them the responsibility for maintaining it) by enfranchising black Southerners. With the vote it was believed would go power sufficient to hold the body politic in a safe place. The Freedmen's Bureau was given the assignment of registering freedmen—but not the freedwomen—to vote.

When Samuel Roberts got to the head of the table where he was to sign his name so that he could vote, he was told no. Born in 1849, he was only eighteen and too young. But Peter Maxwell, who had fought in the United States Army, was not, and neither was Thomas Bailey, who was born in the eighteenth century; they registered. Two years out of slavery, the people who had come back to Sapelo to make it theirs were eager to protect their possession of themselves as well as to affirm their place in that strange larger society that, by giving them the vote, was acknowledging that place.

Tunis Campbell, from his headquarters in Darien—
and a black man at that—urged the men of the hammocks
on Sapelo to register, and the formal rules were all
observed. The very signing was a secular ritual of belonging. Samuel Roberts had the eagerness to come into the
company of the elect; his only problem was being a
teenager.

March and Prince Carter were not. They, fifty and
forty-six, registered saying they had lived in McIntosh
County all their lives.[2] One after another, the men of the
island either put their recently learned skill in writing to
work or relied on the familiar if vaguely demeaning "X,"
and added their names—Abram Spaulding, Henry Lewis,
James Lemon (another veteran), Thomas Bailey, Sampson Hogg (using the name Hall), Perault Dixon—to the
register and, later, took themselves to the ballot box.

That long registration list is a roll of honor. The ritual
of election did not prevent its desecration by white
supremacists four decades later, but those who took away
the vote were not able to rub those names from the historical memory. In 1867, there was no thought in the island
voters' minds that their revolution would turn so firmly
backward. That year, and the few just after it, black Georgians were more active politically than they were to be for
a century. At an April Republican convention in Darien,
Campbell not only exhorted the freedmen present to vote,
but initiated a petition to General John Pope, the federal
general supervising the Freedmen's Bureau's registration
efforts, to quicken the process. In May he was in Macon
for the Georgia education convention that addressed the
need for local involvement in the drive to improve the
schools—and find teachers for them. In June, he was a

delegate to the remarkable conference in Augusta called by the African Methodist Episcopal Zion Church.[3]

There was no line between the sacred and the secular in that Zion chapel. The Zion branch of Methodism was black America's own; unlike the African Methodist Church, it had not begun under the auspices of the larger white denomination. And there was a new Georgia, a new nation, to be built. Every aspect of political participation was discussed, as was the need to inform the black citizenry of its rights and to insist on their exercise. Campbell, impressed by the unequivocal radical call for full equality in the local *Augusta Daily Loyal Georgian*, came away from this rousing meeting both a contributing editor of the national *Zion Standard and Weekly* and even more determinedly political.[4] The Augusta meeting was a rousing call to action; it terrified most of white Georgia.

In time that terror turned back on the Augusta and Sapelo optimists. Not only was Tunis Campbell driven out of the considerable power that he had amassed in McIntosh County (and even put on a chain gang, following dubious legal processes), but, by the century's end, even the steadily diminished opportunities for black participation in their own governing—as justices of the peace and clerks in governmental offices—were lost. And finally, in 1906, they were legally disenfranchised.

African-Americans' anger may derive as much from the broken promises of Reconstruction as from slavery itself. So much promise was held out, so much withdrawn, that the sting is still there. Slavery had promised nothing. What sustained the slaves then was what they created for themselves, hindered or abetted capriciously by their masters. Then, with emancipation and Reconstruction, official, public promises were made—and broken. Expectations rose and were dashed; psychological damage was done. The rug was pulled out from under them; during slavery there had been no rug.

Simply by voting, Reconstruction Sapelo had not achieved the power to make its world work, and the reenfranchised Sapelo people today know that the vote still offers no such guarantee. But, as Americans everywhere have an annual—or at least quadrennial—new burst of hope, on election day, the people of Sapelo come down to the community center to vote.

The community center lacks centrality. Nudged barely inside Hog Hammock just as the road ceases to be paved, it is in its newness a building that wandered in and couldn't find a comfortable place to sit. It's a pretty building, but not at home; it's a suburban subdivision version of a modest Mississippi planter's house that tentatively walked into the party, felt a little unwelcome, and took a seat along the wall, but under a comforting oak.

Its redemption is its wide porch along the front wall, wrapping around one side. In a sturdy row of rocking chairs, the old people sit waiting for the daily hot meal and greeting their fellows who climb out of pickups and make for the steps.

One day sitting in a rocker on the porch, I was chatting with two men visiting from Savannah. At that moment, one of the older men of the island arrived, and looking hard at one of the strangers, he said, "You must be a Lemon." Laughing, James Lemon allowed as how you couldn't get away with anything on Sapelo.

On election day, a good many of Sapelo's people climb those steps. Cornelia Bailey, the registrar now, proudly recalls that when Georgia's Jimmy Carter was elected president in 1976, 100 percent of the registered men and women cast their ballots. When she reaches the table, Madeline Carter's name is on the register that her grandfather, Samuel Roberts, had not been allowed to sign—in 1867—simply because he was too young.

In 1993, a few months after they had helped choose another president of the United States, the Sapelo voters were back again on the more urgent business of electing a new sheriff for McIntosh County. Two decades ago, that post had been held by Tom Poppell, one of the most notorious—and most original—of Georgia's long list of autocratic county sheriffs. Since his reign, several men, white men, had worn the badge; now the Sapelo voters were, for the fourth time, at the ballot box trying to complete the selection of a new sheriff. There had been three previous ballots—the primary, the runoff primary, which Charles Jones had won by two contested votes, and the regular November election, when a vote for him could not, by court order, be counted—and now, finally, there was a decisive election. The time had come. For this last ballot, Jones's people made sure to turn out, and, by a handy margin, McIntosh County had, for the first time in this century, a black sheriff.

Charles—Chunk—Jones is a great-great-grandson of both Alonzo B. Guyton, deputy sheriff during Reconstruction and then, into the mid-1890s, McIntosh County's longtime sheriff, and the first Charles Jones, who, with his wife, Rose Bailey Jones, lived on Sapelo through that earlier better of times.[5]

The regaining of the franchise, then, has given the islanders more than simply a long-overdue restoration of self-esteem. But no Sapelo voters today would put as much faith in the ballot box as did their forebears in the heady days of Reconstruction. Black Southerners then were to learn that the vote was not sufficient protection from deprivation of their rights, including that of the franchise itself.

If today Sapelo's people are older and wiser, they are still dangerously vulnerable to the decisions of those off the island with vastly greater power. The vote is no warrant for letting down the guard. Cornelia Bailey has the energy, the determination, that was so much in the air in 1865, 1866, 1867. For the people then, though they did not know it at the time, the barriers to be put in the way of achieving all that should have been theirs were even higher than those lying in Cornelia and her neighbors' path now. But morning-after futility sets in soon after election day.

All the many things that have not worked out in the past cloud proud hopes for the future. But those hopes won't down; there are good people, some with power, who sometimes listen. Like Tunis Campbell, Cornelia Bailey is always on her way to another meeting to plead, to demand, to scorn, to lament—to be heard.

9

Raccoon Bluff

The end was there from the beginning. Sapelo's people were back on their island, but that island was not wholly to be theirs. They had their school, their church, even their ballot box, but the land—ten thousand acres of arable land into which large prosperous farms could have been dug—was denied them. It had been promised, and initially the promise was acted on. Farms were established and crops planted, but these gains under General Sherman's order, which stated that the "islands . . . are reserved and set apart for the settlement of the negroes," that "on the islands, no white person, unless military . . . will be permitted to reside,"[1] scarcely outlasted the war the black Georgians had thought they had won.

Those victors did not yield easily. As one of the family recalled, the Spaldings "sent a representative to the Island to take possession for the owners. But give it up? No indeed! When ordered to leave, the negroes declared the land was theirs, and in turn ordered Mr. Bass to leave, threatening to kill him if he did not go. And go he did, there being nothing else to do."[2]

There was, in fact, a good deal more to be done once the vanquished decided they had not been. And "Mr. Bass"—Allen G. Bass—along with his sister, Mary Bass Spalding, and her other relatives, were busy doing it. When the war ended, Mary Spalding, a widow since Randolph Spalding's death in Savannah, from disease, in the spring of 1862, came back to McIntosh County, to her mainland house in The Ridge, across the channels from Sapelo. If the family's bank account had been in Confederate funds, she was strapped for cash, and their assets in land, on the island, were in the hands of some of their other assets—once worth close to a million dollars—their former slaves.

It was this Spalding widow, acting for herself and her three children, who had sent her brother on his momentarily futile mission. When it failed, the family regrouped, and, as proved true in many cases across the South, it was the woman in the family who led the often successful fight to regain one of the assets, the land, and to attempt to regain control of the others, the freedpeople. (As William Faulkner said, "the men had given in . . . but the women had never surrendered.")[3] Mary Bass Spalding was at the barricades in a counterrevolution.

Americans would not have been unique if, as a result of the revolution that the Civil War had been, there had been redistribution of land in favor of the people who had worked, rather than owned, it. And, indeed, such a reassigning of lands had been underway along the Carolina and Georgia coast since the arrival of the Union Navy in 1861. In May 1865, the Freedmen's Bureau divided 390 of the thousands of acres of land that Thomas Spalding—Mary's son—had inherited from his grandfather and namesake into plots ranging in size from fifteen to forty acres. These farm lots were granted to Fergus Wilson and fourteen other freedmen heads of household.[4] John Williams was one of the farmers whose warrant was for acreage on what had been "A. M. Kennan's [Catherine Spalding Kenan's husband's] Hanging Bull Plant'n Sapelo I[slan]d."[5] Williams appears to have settled on the land and begun farming before the warrant was issued. Jack Hillary was granted twenty acres on "R. Spaulding P'n 'South End' "; scores of other families had similar plots.[6] The freed people who had sent Bass packing were taking the act of Congress of March 3, 1865, seriously: ". . . and to every male citizen, whether refugee or freedman . . . there shall be assigned not more than forty acres of such land."[7]

The word "ours" hovered angrily over Sapelo. The land which Allen Bass had futilely demanded be returned was the ground into which farmers had planted those seeds that Tunis Campbell had worked so hard to supply the previous spring. Those crops, this land, were "ours," the farmers thought. On the other hand, the Spaldings, like hundreds of other planter families of similar determination and with no shortage of useful connections, were determined to circumvent Congress's legislation and make those lands "ours"—again.

A few of the Freedmen's Bureau officials were determined to enforce the law. In July 1865, Rufus Saxton and his aides in the Freedmen's Bureau for South Carolina, Georgia, and Florida posted two hundred copies of an invitation, Saxton's Circular 1, to inform heads of households who had not yet gotten warrants that they too might be awarded forty acres of the lands abandoned on the islands and coastal mainland.[8] Applicants were assured that these grants would be made under the direct authorization of the act creating the Freedmen's Bureau.

On Sapelo, Tunis Campbell saw Saxton's new order as ratification of the redistribution of land that had already taken place. And, for the moment, it looked as if they had the support of Washington in this endeavor. General O. O. Howard, the commissioner of the bureau, ordered agents, like Campbell, to "with as little delay as possible, select, and set apart such confiscated and abandoned land . . . as may be deemed necessary for the immediate use of Refugees and freedmen. . . ." These tracts were to be divided "into lots . . . according to the law establishing the Bureau."[9]

Unfortunately for the freedmen, fortunately for Mary Spalding and her relatives, President Andrew Johnson thought poorly of that law. Rather than responding to his constitutional duty to uphold it, he nullified it by exercising his power of pardon. On May 29, he had issued his Amnesty Proclamation, and, in a series of orders throughout the summer of 1865, he extended the terms of Confederate pardons to include the return of lands that had been abandoned. And yet, through that summer, Saxton and Freedmen's Bureau agents siding with the black farmers held firm against displacing farmers from lands already granted and continued making new grants.

The first major act of destruction of the redistribution plan came in the fall of 1865, when General Howard, responding to the president's wishes, went south to plead with the freedpeople to give up the thought of being independent farmers. Instead, they were to go to work for former masters and other landowners. His rhetoric suggested that to do so was to accept an equally good definition of what freedom meant. The Freedmen's Bureau was an adjunct of the army, and conservative army officers, who were legion, were as anxious as the president to replace men like Saxton and Campbell; even Howard, a senior officer in the army, was wary of being fired.

In September, Howard, to placate the president, removed Saxton from jurisdiction over the bureau in mainland Georgia (but not yet the islands) and appointed in his place General Davis Tillson. In Tennessee, Tillson had earned the confidence of landowners: "The chaotic condition of the labor system is being reduced to order."[10] As one conservative newspaper reported, the bureau in that state, under his direction, provided "employers the means of compelling the fulfillment of engagements on the part of the employee."[11]

These "employees" were the former slaves who were compelled to work for planters who either had never left their lands or had regained them. Now Tillson was to bring this policy of forcing the freedpeople to work under contracts to Georgia. But first, he had to see to it that the potential "employers" had lands restored to them so that the employing could take place. The Spaldings had yet to achieve that restoration on Sapelo; the two men who, along with some determined farmers, stood in their way were Rufus Saxton and Tunis Campbell.

Through the fall of 1865, Saxton, acutely aware that "the high toned chivalry"[12] were putting pressure on President Johnson to force him out, steadfastly refused to abandon the freedpeople of the sea islands: "On this soil they and their ancestors passed two hundred years of unremitting toil."[13] He refused to ask for a transfer away from the islands. He held out until January 1866, when, curtly, he was ordered out of the Freedmen's Bureau. In his place, Tillson was given jurisdiction over all of Georgia—including the islands.

Campbell tried to enlist Tillson's cooperation in assisting the freedpeople as independent farmers, but the general turned the tables on him. Traveling to Sapelo with Campbell, Tillson endeavored to capitalize on the trust which Campbell had earned with "the colored people." It was Toby Maxwell, one of the island farmers, who reported on the meeting. In a deposition in Campbell's behalf when a commission of the Georgia senate was hearing charges that Campbell had disturbed the racial "harmony" of McIntosh County, Maxwell stated that he "had known Mr. Campbell since 1865 on Sapalo Island." Maxwell insisted that Campbell, far from causing racial strife, had been serving as "adviser" on "how to live."[14]

At the 1865 meeting, Tillson required Campbell to stand aside and introduced S. D. Dickson and his partner, named McBride, who had, for $2,500, rented the south end lands from the Spaldings, who claimed they owned them.[15] The two Northerners had come determined to make the black occupants of the lands sign sharecropping contracts for cotton they were already raising. Even had they been satisfied with the offered two-thirds share of the profit from the sale of the cotton, the farmers, by signing, would be acknowledging that they did not own the land on which they were growing the crop.

Dickson and McBride also opened a store on the island, from which the freedpeople would have to buy provisions—on credit, with repayment to be subtracted from the farmers' share of the profit on the cotton. Tillson insisted that the black people sign these contracts; later, privately, Campbell, no doubt dispirited, cautioned the farmers "that they must be careful how they made contracts . . . if they violated them they would be put in prison."[16] Hoping that sharecropping would not last, he suggested that the men contract "by the week or by the month so as not to get themselves involved with the white people." Despite the warnings, most if not all of the farmers working those lands did sign contracts.

Another freedman, Samuel Ross, attested that he had "always heard" Campbell "convincing the col[ored] people to work and live honest, [to] try to be harmonious with the white people, that if they expected to be respected they must respect themselves . . . [the] true policy was to live in harmony one with the other."[17] But harmony did not prevail. Toby Maxwell, having reluctantly made a contract and delivered his cotton to the store for sale, reported that McBride and Dickson "stole everything the col[ored] men made & that this stealing and outrage was done by the direction of Genl Tilson." Maxwell claimed that when his "cotton was taken" by the two men, he "owed them nothing," and protested when he was not paid for it. Others of the "col[ored] men" then "refused to put their cotton in McBride's pile."[18]

Furious, McBride, who had no soldiers at his elbow, sent word to Tillson, who supplied them. Then, as Tillson reported to his superior officer, General Howard, commissioner of the Freedmen's Bureau, his men arrested "12 of the ringleaders and confine[d] them in Fort Pulaski where they will be kept at hard labor until such times as they shall have made up their minds to return to the island and conduct themselves as becomes peaceful law abiding citizens."[19] Toby Maxwell was chained, transported, and jailed in the bleak fortress which throughout the war had stood as a symbol of Confederate rebellion against the nation in the army of which his brother had fought.[20]

The Spaldings also wanted to go home to Sapelo. They did not want simply to rent or sell land for needed cash, they sought to return to the island to live. But they were not willing to do so as long as there were so many threatening black people sharing the island with them. General Tillson had his headquarters in Augusta, up the Savannah River, but when he visited the city of Savannah, Mary Spalding saw to it that he had a caller. Her brother-in-law, Charles Spalding, made a trip from The Ridge to Savannah to meet with Tillson. Spalding's "supplication to the General" was not in vain; the vanquished Confederate saw to it that his conqueror did his bidding.[21]

As one of the members of the family recorded, Tillson "sent a detachment of U.S. troops with Mr. Spalding to Sapelo."[22] The member of the family who accompanied the troops was Catherine Spalding Kenan's husband, Michael Kenan. Like Allen Bass before him, Kenan ran into opposition—this time from Toby Maxwell, returned but unrepentant. As Maxwell recalled it in his deposition, "Mr. Kenion [Kenan] the owner of the island told [me] that his people [his family] was coming & he wanted . . . [my] place."[23]

Toby Maxwell went to Darien to appeal to Tunis Campbell, who in turn protested to the Freedmen's

Bureau in Washington, but to no avail. Tillson's federal troops, as a member of the Spalding family recorded, "dispossessed the negroes, and turned the property over to the rightful owners. All negroes but the Spalding people were made to leave then and there."[24]

Maxwell was forced from Sapelo along with upward of six hundred people—roughly ninety families: "Genl Tilson . . . ordered them off the Island & they had no place of their own to go to."[25] They had neither land nor jobs, but unlike other similarly displaced freedpeople, these once-again refugees had a champion. Maxwell, himself later an alderman in Darien, credited Tunis Campbell with having "procured provisions for the col-[ored] people," who, having left the island in a flotilla of small boats that Campbell was forced to assemble, came away with nothing.[26]

Campbell, seeking to fight back against the injustice to his fellow black citizens and determined to establish a political base in McIntosh County, entered into "a rent-to-own agreement for a 1,250 acre plantation, Belle Ville." There he established " 'the Belle Ville Farmer's Association,' the members of which grew marketable crops to pay the lease."[27] Some, but only a few, of those driven from the island became part of this promising agricultural experiment.

The people expelled from Sapelo were, in the eyes of the Spalding family, "vagrant runaway negroes" who had "taken possession . . . during the war." The Kenans and Spaldings felt no obligation to them, but did toward the "Spalding negroes" who had "flocked back as soon after emancipation as possible. Sapelo being the Mecca of their desires." They were permitted to remain in their hammocks—but lost whatever of the former Spalding lands they had been farming.

Presumably, the Spaldings, moving back to the island, assumed that these people of theirs would want to go back to work in the old way. If hoped-for ancient loyalty would not inspire this, then perhaps the Freedmen's Bureau would again lend a hand. That was not the job that Agent Campbell thought he had been given, but he was fast losing his ability to protect the freedpeople. And soon he lost his job—and turned to politics. It took Tillson a year to fire Campbell, but finally in 1867 he managed to find him guilty of "misconduct" and dismissed him from the bureau.

Campbell's replacement for Sapelo was Allen G. Bass. Now it was all in the family, and former slaves were to become current laborers. Or so their former masters thought. But the Spaldings misjudged the sway of paternalism. Surely, they thought, their people would once again work the cotton fields they had once worked, would help reinvent the old world of deference to the big house.

They thought wrongly. As far as I can determine, after the war no Spalding made money on a crop of Sapelo cotton. Pride alone had been served by the regaining of the land; when half a century later the last of the once rich family's holdings were sold, they went for a song. Had the white families acquiesced to the grant—or even sale—of farming lands to the black families, had they been satisfied from the start with the living and working arrangements which, in fact, were to be theirs as long as they resided on Sapelo—hiring neighbors for specific tasks in the pasturelands and woodlots—there would have been a better prospect for modest prosperity for all of the island's people, black and white.

Even without plots of prime land, the black farmers did not yield their independence. Not only did they successfully avoid contracting to work in field gangs, but apparently they escaped sharecropping as well. McBride and Dickson fade from the record; it would appear that not even Agent Bass could (or perhaps wanted to) persuade black farmers to work for the two. They were gone from the island by the time of the census of 1870. Sapelo's people, no longer the "Spalding negroes," held on to their homeplaces and subsisted on the vegetables raised in garden plots and on meat from their hogs and meat and eggs from their chickens—and the abundant (and nutritious) fish they caught.

The Spaldings did indeed move back; all three of Mary and Randolph Spalding's children and their spouses lived there from 1871 until 1885 in three houses along Barn Creek—one on an exquisite point looking out toward the northward reach of Doboy Sound.[28] There were Kenan cousins on the island as well. They lived in simple houses—which they loved—but their grandfather's big house at the south end was left as it had been during the war, abandoned.

In 1870 the census taker counted fifty-nine families living in the hammocks along with the returned Spaldings, Mary Bass Spalding, her sons, Thomas and Bourke, and their wives, her daughter, Sarah, and Sarah's husband. Collectively, the members of the family were listed as owning $33,000 of real estate. Not one of the hammock families was considered to own real estate of any value.[29] The census taker was hewing to the line drawn when Davis Tillson, with Agent Bass's good assistance, had denied ownership of the Sherman-grant lands to the freed-people. But the people he was counting recalled the general's award. The nation, they thought, had given its word; it may yet be called on to keep it.

The others sharing the island were James Thompson, "planter" (who rented Spalding land) and his wife and "Geo. W. Kinsbury," a "carpenter" living with them. There were also Thomas Heson, a ship's carpenter, and John Smith, a pilot, both of whom apparently lived in close proximity to the Spaldings, and, finally, James C. Clark and Montgomery Styles, the keepers of the lighthouse that still stands at the island's extreme southern tip.[30]

In 1873, Randolph Spalding's large holdings in the north half of the island were sold to one Northerner, then to another, and finally to a third, Amos Sawyer, a soap manufacturer from Northampton, Massachusetts.[31] Each of these men hoped to make a fortune raising cotton as old Thomas Spalding had once done. But all failed. The Spaldings meanwhile had turned to lumbering and raising beef cattle. Families left the island and returned, mortgages were taken and foreclosed, and by the century's end the only relic of the once lordly clan was Sarah Spalding McKinley, who, having moved back to Milledgeville for a time, returned, with her husband, Archibald C. McKinley, to become the island's postmistress.

Economically, everyone had been the loser in the land restoration policy that the Spaldings had insisted on. It would have taken only a little over half of the arable land on the island to provide the 130 families with forty-acre farms; instead, most of it went back to thicket and then to forest. The forty-five heads of household in 1870 worked

farms averaging only eleven acres in size; they were farming only 502 "improved acres."[32] Each of the farms was
worth scarcely more than $40, and the average worth of a
farmer's tools was only $12.44. There were five horses and
nine mules for the farmers to use; there was record of only
a single cow to give milk, while, not going far to balance
the diet, there were ninety-seven hogs, two per household.

The farmers were raising thirty-nine bushels of corn,
thirty-three bushels of peas and beans, and twenty-seven
bushels of sweet potatoes per household, and four of the
farmers were raising rice—1,320 pounds were produced
in the prior year. If to this the rich supply of easily caught
fish is added, the subsistence of the islanders was achieved.
When it came to cash, the seventy-three bales of cotton
sold at the end of the 1869 season would have yielded, at
the top of the market, only $40.15.[33]

In 1871, three Sapelo men met the land possessors on
their own terms in an effort to establish a more orderly
stretch of farmlands than the backyard plots. William Hillery, John Grovner, and Bilally Bell organized a land
company and, pooling a $500 down payment, which they
had, somehow, amassed, purchased one thousand acres
in Raccoon Bluff for $2,000. They paid $500 on signing
the purchase agreement and gave notes for $500 due on
each of the next three firsts of January.[34]

Having secured this good, dry, high land, they did not,
however, have the wherewithal to keep the tract intact
and, collectively, farm it on a reasonably large scale.
Instead, it appears that each of the three took about 111
acres for himself and then divided the remaining 666 acres

into twenty plots of roughly thirty-three acres apiece. The purchasers of these plots, all save two of whom bore surnames still current on the island, moved to the northwest of the island from Hanging Bull and other hammocks, and at Raccoon Bluff established the most ambitious of the island's communities.[35]

The Raccoon Bluff community sustained itself for three-quarters of a century. In time, it had at its center the handsome First African Baptist Church when that congregation moved from its down-island location in about 1899. By then there were twenty-five or thirty houses in the hammock and farmers grew peas, rice, potatoes, and sugarcane and raised hogs for meat and lard. When Allen Green was a boy, there was a three-room school in Raccoon Bluff, complete with a teacher not afraid to use a strap. Boys sat on one side of a classroom, girls on the other, but, he recalls, they got together during recess.

Allen Green was born in Raccoon Bluff in "nineteen aught seven," and it was there, when he was eleven, that his grandfather gave him his instruction in basketmaking. And it was from the foot of the bluff that he and other boys would swim across to Blackbeard Island and walk round to the ocean side to ride the waves.

Life on the bluff, if measured in other than cash terms, was rich. But if one of the Raccoon Bluff boys, from a vantage point as remote as the Atlantic Coast has to offer, grew curious about the world on the mainland, he might be tempted, as Allen was, to get up and go have a look. At eighteen, Allen Green did—and found his way to Florida. He doesn't talk much about those days—he was away for fourteen years—except to recall having once walked from Miami to Jacksonville, a trek that far outstripped that of his grandfather coming back to Sapelo after the Civil War.

In 1880, the census taker's findings suggest the initial success of the land company. Now sixteen of the Sapelo men owned land, while twenty-two were now recorded as tenants holding their places "for fixed money rental."[36] Absent records, it can be guessed that some of the rental payments were in the form of payments on the purchase of plots from the land company while the remaining families lived on house plots that averaged only 6.2 acres each and that had been theirs back in the days of slavery.

The poverty that had set in after the Civil War did not lose its hold on the island's people, black or white. The impecunious McKinleys—she a stooped, white-haired old lady, he a long-white-bearded Confederate veteran—died in 1916 and 1917, fifty years after the birth and death of their only child. There were no more white Spaldings on the island. The land, as property, had been restored to their family, but it had not produced prosperity for them or for any of the white possessors to which they sold it.

It would be nice to be able to record that the Hillery land company was the beginning of agricultural prosperity for a good many of the Sapelo families, but it was not. I can find no record of the long-term successful marketing of money crops. On the other hand, there were individual enterprises—an oyster shucking and packing plant, a sawmill—but none of the islanders' businesses lasted. It was as if Sapelo, having expelled the money-makers, wouldn't allow what the rest of America thought of as the right kind of entrepreneurship to take hold on its sacred sand. As her people somehow understand, you do with her only what she has to offer—her oysters, her trees for lumbering. And her demands for respect.

That respect is paid today by a couple of islanders who

have combined ingenuity with a recognition that Sapelo still beckons to explorers. Caesar Banks, a cousin of James Banks and James Jr., left the island, became a master of tabby construction, and plied his trade on nearby St. Simons Island. He returned with his wife, Nancy; when I am on the island I kid her about being Sapelo's other outsider. The two live in a house faced with Caesar's tabby. There is, off to the side, a short trail leading down to the tag end of a tidal creek which, at high tide, provides enough water to allow a small skiff to work its way through the marsh and to the sea.

That marsh, framed by the Bankses' oaks, seems to stretch forever. Birds darting low over the endless grass alone give motion to the emptiness of the marsh's sweep. The silence is broken in the most unlikely way; the Bankses have two of the most ridiculous of all fowl, peacocks, gaudy and raucous. Caesar is a confessed collector—of cars, gear of all sorts, and the two vans in which he transports guests from the dock and around the island. He and Nancy are the efficient proprietors of their island version of a bed-and-breakfast.

Once on a second Sunday, I walked to St. Luke's with the two of them. Nancy is an exceedingly pretty woman; pretty is exactly the word. Her dress is an almost purple blue and an almost red purple; her hat tan; like those of the other ladies her high-heeled shoes are black patent leather. Caesar, portly, is packed into the men's uniform, a three-piece dark blue suit. On the way down I have the wit to get change for a twenty-dollar bill from Nancy; the public offering, they advise helpfully, is where the bigger bills go, smaller ones are needed for the others. There's practicality; there's a sense of humor.

Mr. and Mrs. Banks, as they enter the church that morning, embody the republic's regard for both self-reliance and respect of community. They are the neighbors who put together the land company at Raccoon Bluff. They are the banished Toby Maxwell.

10

Barn Creek

Sapelo's people were many—539 in 1910—and busy, but their independence was once more at risk. In 1912, Howard Coffin, with the wherewithal of one of the earliest of the great automobile fortunes—he was an engineer who designed for four of the turn-of-the-century manufacturers, including the Olds Motor Works and the Hudson Motor Car Company—repeated Thomas Spalding's feat of creating a barony on the island. Shrewdly, working with David Crenshaw Barrow, Jr., an able lawyer and a relative of the many financially straitened Spalding heirs, he bought all of their holdings, as well as those held by the heirs of Amos Sawyer.

Coffin was as energetic an entrepreneur as Thomas Spalding had been a planter. On Sapelo, he wrenched the island into production with as much zeal as Spalding had brought to the job. Much new-growth forest was leveled, a sawmill fed, an oyster-canning plant opened, crops planted, and cattle brought from the mainland to be grazed.

Coffin, like rich Northerners who discovered other islands, was host to curious visitors who found his remote domain both elegant and intriguing. In 1928, President Calvin Coolidge had his portrait painted in Coffin's library in the rebuilt great house at the south end. Charles Lindbergh landed on the airstrip in 1929, the Hoovers were there in 1932, Claire Boothe Brokaw—later Luce—in 1933. The guests' cameras caught the baron's peasantry, picturesque on ox-drawn carts; the era's celebrities could watch a man poke a jaw-testing log at an alligator. For the first visiting president, the host, mixing metaphors, staged a rodeo on the great, wide, flat beach with black cowboys roping steers. Mrs. Coolidge took home movies.

Rose Hillery and Matty Carter were in the kitchen. Matty has no trouble remembering her first days, "when I was coming up," learning to cook in the kitchen of the big house. The pay was "nothing to talk about," but it was at least a salary and not the present-day hourly wage that seems to her and to others demeaning. When she graduated to chief cook—a not minor post, given the table for which she was cooking—she found herself employed by the next arriving baron, Richard J. Reynolds, Jr.

When Coffin's attention, in the thirties, turned to another island and, in the depression, his credit ran short, he sold what he knew as *his* Sapelo to Reynolds, the son of the Winston-Salem tobacco lord. In Reynolds's hands, the south end of the island became a playground, with a movie theater in the stables quadrangle. The big house had already achieved eclectic grandeur; there was the excellent wood paneling of the Coffin library, the less than excellent neo-Roman jug-carrying statues around the outdoor pool. Indoors, behind the huge fireplace of the entryway, was another pool, and now there was the party room, decorated as a circus tent, upstairs, and a bowling alley down—and guest room after guest room. Straight as a die from the front door, the road runs, escaping, to the beach.

These twentieth-century colonial princes ruled but did not conquer. Their power was money, and they had a great deal of money. Like capitalist colonialists the world round, they had the power to exploit and the power with which to be paternalistically benevolent. If Coffin worked his hirelings hard, he also was the person who gave the piano for the dance hall. If Reynolds, finally by threatening to close the road, forced Allen Green out of the last house to be evacuated from Raccoon Bluff so that his wildlife—hunting—preserve, which takes up virtually the whole of the north half of the island, could be complete, the foundation established with his money pays a part of James and Shannon Banks's college expenses.

You can't walk the island or talk of long-ago time—or the present—with any islander without hearing of wrongs wrought. But in the face of dominance from the south end, there had been enterprise of its own in Hog Hammock. Charles Hall, a great-great-grandson of Bilali and a nephew of Shad Hall, was born on Sapelo in 1874 and died in 1974. For years he brought the mail from the mainland—for a time, reportedly, rowing out with it. In later years, he had a car on the mainland to get the mail to his boat at the dock and another on the island. Going back and forth as he did, he was often asked to pick up groceries for his neighbors, which led him to open a store on Sapelo, but all was not well. His wife died; the store failed.

Resilience was not in short supply on Sapelo, and Charles Hall married again in 1933, to Beulah Walker from Raccoon Bluff (Annie Mae Green, Allen Green's wife, is Beulah Walker's youngest sister), and opened another store in his house. This time it worked. Matty Carter recalls it as a place that made Hog Hammock a true village; she laments its closing when Charles Hall died. Hall, with his own generator, had lights not only in the store but in all the rooms of the house. Only a fraction of the other families had electricity when Charles was a boy; after World War II, Richard J. Reynolds had a single line run from his generator up into the community.

Electricity and water lines—even fireplugs appeared—and similarly designed small houses were part of Reynolds's plan to concentrate all of the island's people in one central, inland place—in Hog Hammock. This was part of the come-on as Reynolds began the swap of land outside Hog Hammock for land and houses within it. The people in the north end communities were urged and then coerced into accepting the exchange, on a less-than-acre-for-acre basis. Hicks Walker moved his family down from Belle Marsh, below Chocolate, on the island's west side and settled in the northernmost lot in Hog Hammock. He wasn't going any farther inside than he had to. What was given up was not only waterside holdings for landlocked plots, but also what had been home for the whole of long lives.

If Coffin and Reynolds had money and power, the islanders had virtually no money and none of what the world understands as power. There is no denying that they were dependent first on Coffin and then on Reynolds, as now they are on the public heirs of those private landholders, the state of Georgia's Department of Natural

Resources and its University of Georgia. Reynolds left most of his holdings, including his ill-defined forest preserve, to the state, which stands as the preserve's precarious guardian. As long as there are governors and commissioners who respect the unique and truly invaluable natural resource that the island is, real estate and recreational predators are held at bay. But governors and commissioners can change. Some arrangement more solid than that presently existing is needed to hold the line; some changes are underway.

One provision of any national or state conservation park that would protect from development the immense beauty of the island should be the preservation of Hog Hammock. Each resident should be assured that the community will not be subject to the will of whoever circled Hog Hammock on one official's map and marked it "to be acquired." Rather, each holding should be guaranteed to the present residents or their descendants, in perpetuity. There are precedents for this now on Indian lands and for householders in areas incorporated into national parks. And even if there were not, Sapelo's people have earned through tenacity if through nothing else the right, the rightness, of having their island.

But this is not the story of that battle or of the many past battles that living Sapelo people, not without bitterness, recall fighting to maintain their hold. As Cornelia Bailey puts it, we don't need a sign "that says 'Hog Hammock *Was* Here,' " we want a sign that says " 'Hog Hammock *Is* Here.' "[1] I am not afraid of battles, but in Behavior, at least, they seem aside from why I am on Sapelo. As I told Matty Carter one of the first times we talked, it was the people of Hog Hammock themselves

whom I wanted to know and not those who looked after
or threatened them. And what, in return, I hoped I could
give back to her was a longer-ago long-ago time than that
of her long memory.

I have tried to tell of the American past of these African
Americans who as slaves and then as freedpeople allowed
their Sapelo the liberty of making them her own. But the
story of these long twentieth-century years, years within
the memory of Sapelo's people, is not the story that I came
back to the island to tell. I came not to interrogate, but
to visit. I was there not to master the intricate, delicate
diplomatic negotiations attendant on the community's
painful efforts to survive, but, instead, to try to grasp its
domestic tranquillities. The pain of loneliness, of uncer-
tainty, of old age lies beneath its quiet, of course. There
are, after all, only sixty-seven people left in Hog Hammock. But what strikes you over and over again is the
duration of their story, of their endurance.

Of course there had been vast change since Thomas
Spalding hauled his wild Africans onto the island as slaves,
these slaves who became free, and, free, learned that freedom can be held captive to poverty. Freedom can be
inched in on in other ways as well by outsiders meaning
well or thinking ill. Sapelo's people have experienced too
many other people doing for them; they want, as they
always have, to do for themselves. And what seems so
immensely difficult for any but themselves to see is how
well they have done.

And so, it seems to me, all that I should do, all that I
can do in return for what I have learned on their island,
is to give back to Sapelo's people a bit of the past that lies
beyond the scope of memory—the days of great-grand-

mothers' great-grandmothers are, inevitably, being lost to time. If, with that other remembering that is history, I can rebuild a bit of that long past, I will feel I have earned my walk in Behavior. When it is crafted, it will be the basket that I will leave along its sand road.

Two great storms frame the Sapelo past that I have come to know, the hurricanes of 1824 and 1898. Ravaging storms are major events on the vulnerable low-slung sea islands. The pounding ocean is bass to the falsetto shriek of relentless wind. And what the wind doesn't blow over or away can be carried off by waves, unimpeded by the four-foot-high dunes, overreaching the vast stretches of the island's flat center. Hurricanes come often and do their damage, but near-yearly terrors are ordinary compared to those of 1824 and 1898.

Many accounts remain of the first of these storms which devastated Sapelo and her sister islands. There were "great masses of black and beetling clouds" forced ahead of fierce winds and splashed round with the "play and gleam of lightning."[2] Then a lull, then violence as trees crashed in every direction. Again, as the eye of the storm passed over the island, there was another break of thirty minutes until the storm raced back more violently than before. The sea crashed in, covering the whole of the island. There was terrible loss of property along the Georgia coast—all of Sapelo's crops were lost and cattle drowned—and worse loss of human lives. The *Savannah Georgian*, full of stories of destruction, reported that "Mrs. Lafong, a widow lady of Patterson Island, and whole of her negroes, were swept away by the water and drowned."[3]

On Sapelo, the big house held through the harrowing night: "When dawn came the sun arose on a morning clear and calm. . . . A runner from the Barn Creek settlement made his way . . . to say all was well; that BuAllah [Bilali], head foreman of the plantation, had the day before given orders to each of the drivers to take every man, woman, and child to the tabby cotton and sugar houses; that all had been taken to those two-storied and safe refuges; that not a life had been lost and that the water was fast falling."[4]

By 1898, those strong tabby structures were roofless ruins. The hurricane of that fall is about the earliest event that the oldest of Sapelo's people can recollect. One report of the day tells of waves twelve feet high breaking across a field well over on the west side of the island, away from the ocean. While the husband braced himself against the door to prevent the water from swamping the house, his wife, in thigh-deep water, grabbed a slat from a bed docked at the wall, found (miraculously) two nails, and, slipping her foot under a handle of a flatiron, retrieved it from the hearth. Using the iron for a hammer, she wedged the slat into place as a brace to help secure the door.

Not everyone's house held. Buildings like those at Marsh Landing were destroyed, as was the dock itself. Describing the "greate truble," James Walker reported: "Everything we had is gone from us and leave us nothing only what we can gather out of the woods." His buggy, with which he had met visitors to the island, "is smash up I am lik a fish out of watter." He told too that one "hole family is drown." Walker, his pregnant wife, and their three children under three survived—how, he does not say.[5]

The great live oaks saved others; Mae Ruth Green recalls dignified Sylvia Dunham Wilson telling of being taken up onto the branches of a huge steady oak (that still stands in her yard) when just a tiny girl and watching parts of houses, with animals aboard, being swept past her. This time it was trees and not tabby barns that saved the survivors.

Mrs. Annie Walker is one of them.[6] She was seven years old when the storm hit, and I had wanted to ask if she remembered the day. But we hadn't been introduced and she seemed always to be surrounded by her ladies-in-waiting when I was on Sapelo for the May anniversary. (She lives on the other side now.) Just seeing her told a story of its own. She is tall, slim, and regal in dark blue silk; her white, low-crowned, softly rolled broad-brimmed hat is straight and true on her head. Steadied as she goes, she makes her way onto the *Sapelo Queen* on its way back to the mainland on a bright Sunday afternoon. When in one service the preacher, in salute, called on her relatives to stand, half the congregation rose. All of those standing were descendants of survivors of the 1898 hurricane.

The first of the two great storms came early in the curve of the nineteenth century; the second marked its close. The century had been an arch with freedom as its proud keystone. It had begun in the terror of the almost-silence of a people thought of by another people to be "wild Africans." These new Americans had allowed the island to which they had been cruelly taken to take them in, they had made their homes there, prayed there. And two long generations along they had been marched away slaves— and walked back free, a freedom some of them had fought to win.

Freedom was school and church, for the men, for a time, the vote; it made the family secure. And with that freedom came the promise that the land of their island that they had for lifetimes worked would now be theirs. The promise was broken and freedom itself was bent as a restricting poverty had its way. But on their own, in their hammocks, Sapelo's people held their own. They still do.

The day of the First African Baptist Church anniversary had been calm and clear, only edging up on the insufferable sultry heat that blankets the island in summer. A good deal of the time, in fact, the ease of the weather on Sapelo seems to mock the terrible vulnerability of a barrier island much as life in Hog Hammock makes light of mainland hatred. This had occurred to me one chilled day during the winter following the anniversary.

I left a borrowed van at the "No two-wheel-drive vehicles beyond this point" sign and headed off for Cabretta beach. The road moves out from under the trees and the vast marsh stretches far in both directions as you reach the plank bridge across. A party with three bundled-up little children is fishing in the inlet; I cut left through the trees, up to the grassy knoll, then down through the brush—the trail is closing in—and across the wet spot on a few flimsy scraps of lumber out through the dunes and onto the glaring white beach.

The sun now is shirt-off warm. Slumped against a bit of would-be dune, I see nothing but everything before me. Two flying pelicans, clumsily cruising the quiet water just beyond the surf edge, depart. I'm alone with the width and stretch of a classically blue sea and with a sense of taking stock. Why is it that I don't feel like a stranger here? I'm a long way from where a good many people would say I belong.

This tight little island ought to be a barrier that cannot be broken through. But when you come to know it, you realize that its standing alone, its difference from even the closest of the many Americas across on the mainland, operates not to repel. In a quiet, almost unarticulated way, Sapelo sends a signal. Don't come over here to categorize us, to pack us away into irrelevant quaintness, but do come on over if, with your otherness, you are willing to know us in our singular way—and not make light of the memories we live with.

At first blush, Sapelo would seem to be the categorizer's dream. It would be hard to think of a place in America where the singularity of a group is more in evidence than here. The people are uniformly, uniquely deep Sapelo chestnut brown and are, so many of them, descended from a single African ancestor who resolutely practiced his Muslim faith. Their pickups crisscross lands their relatives worked as slaves. In many of their yards is evidence of the poverty that has dogged African Americans from the start.

Here is distinctiveness as big as a billboard. Why doesn't it make more of a difference? Why am I not a stranger here? My skin color is too light; by island standards I'm rich, have a fancy education, and sound funny when I talk. Of course, I'm an outsider. People are curious about me, and, not surprisingly, suspect that I may not be up to much good. And yet I feel almost at home. It is not that I find Sapelo an Eden; there are too many rusted-out cars for that. It is rather that I have been touched by the island's wisdom of ancient stories of troubles.

Sapelo gives the lie to any facile tale of the brotherhood

of man. It demands that we get past the blindness of thinking that, after all, there is no difference caused by poverty, race, and a history of enslavement on one hand, by the smug self-satisfaction of privileged observers of these phenomena on the other. But it does not follow that stories told on sparse porches cannot be heard by visitors who come to listen. Indeed, the very insistence with which they are told is a summons to cross a bridge, to begin a reconciliation, to enter into acts of comprehension and connection.

To live in Hog Hammock is to live a story; there's no one here who doesn't have a hatful of rich memory—a tale of a relative washed from a raft in the hurricane of '98 and saved by clinging to the great brick tower down on Butler's Island. And each of these memories is part of the larger tale that knits its people, that gives them their dignity, their strength. Some—a remarkably large number, in fact—who have left the island have not lost track of that fact. They come back year after year not merely for a dutiful call on left-behind relatives or in pursuit of barbecue (though, in truth, it's probably a bit of both that pulls them); it's a return to stay in touch, to hold tight to their Sapelo's story.

And now that story has a hold on me. In a self-satisfied way, I knew that with my scholarly training I could explore archives and "sources" to provide an armature on which to fix the scattered, solid bones of the receding history. That was fun to do, but the tables were turned. Right here on the island I came to understand better than I ever have before what an exploration of the past, what history, is all about. Sapelo's people know that their story is theirs, that they are never to be acquired as long as they hold to it. They know too that their story, like any good story of the past, is not something possessed, but something passed on. And hearing, we are drawn into it, made responsible to it.

Sapelo may be buffered from some of the world's worst noise, but it is not isolated from our country's ills, not even from those of our benighted cities. I was born in the largest of these and live now in one that is just learning it must calculate its murder rate. For a good many years I have studied the history of the citizens of those cities who suffer most from their violence. Sapelo's people know them too. One man, raised gently to be a model of politeness—"he held doors for us"—when he worked during the summer for the university's Marine Institute would go home in a rage against an unfair world. He found drugs, murdered a deacon for the morning's collection, and may spend the rest of his life in jail. No, Sapelo knows no immunity.

What it does know is something that Henry David Thoreau knew. To walk sanely in this world, you have to know how to put one foot in front of another on grounding you know as yours. On Sapelo, for James Banks, Jr., it's a path through the trees, long, good miles down the beach. For others on the island it is the road under the pickup.

But James, as a student of psychology at his university, knows as well that solid earth can be had by mastering a discipline. When in the quiet of a good talk I ask him why he sometimes thinks of working in a drug program when he gets his degree, he allows as how it's because he's lost friends to that ungrounded quest for escape. As he makes room for himself to go from Sapelo ready to go to work, he allows me—no longer a stranger—to do the same. He has shared his ground with me.

11

Post Office Landing

"It's our boat." Matty Carter's pride climbed out of the telephone reporting on the service on Sunday dedicating *Miss St. Luke.* She's Hog Hammock's reconditioned eight-passenger brightly white vessel, a Hawk, with a two-hundred-horsepower outboard, that was beached outside the church. Tracy Walker, captain of the *Sapelo Queen,* has known for a long time that his neighbors chafe under the stringency of the state's Department of Natural Resources' schedule for the regular ferry service.

Islands need to be gotten off of. On a daily basis, freedom in Hog Hammock is defined as being able to get in your pickup and go. But on an island, a pickup can get you only as far as a dock—by seven o'clock if, for example, you are a second-grader (and got to the dock in the school bus, Cornelia Bailey at the wheel). The five-fifteen sailing from the other side in the evening restricts the adults who would like to work on the mainland but live on the island.

But nothing as practical as school attendance or work

schedules is the true reason for needing the new boat. The *Sapelo Queen* doesn't run on Sundays other than the first, second, and fifth. There are two other Sundays on which to go to church, other times for arriving than those of the state's boat's scheduled runs. Church is the island's event; to come for any other reason is apt to give away the fact that you've come to check up on an elderly relative. It's right to go out to the island to go to church—but you can't go home again—until Monday—because the boat doesn't run that Sunday.

There is another reason why a boat of its own is so important in Hog Hammock, one that everyone is aware of and no one feels a need to discuss. There is no health facility on the island, and emergencies arise. Even before the advent of the new boat, with its good space and reliable motor, there always seemed to be a boat of some kind available when someone had to get to the hospital. I know. On one of my first visits I was hit by a reasonably dangerous infection; on a Sunday morning, thanks to Lula Walker, George Walker, in one of the university's boats, was at the dock for a trip to Meridian. It was not his first such trip; through the haze of fever I can still recall his giving my wife exceedingly precise, accurate—and well-practiced—directions to the Brunswick hospital.

It will likely still be George or Tracy Walker—or Mike Sellers, Tracy's white co-captain of the *Sapelo Queen*, who signed on as the third licensed volunteer—at the helm when *Miss St. Luke* brings the visiting pastor or the returning relative over to the island. Or takes someone in to the doctor. Those passengers won't, or won't seem to be, asking a personal favor. The boat will be theirs, Hog Hammock's. Not everyone contributed to the fund to buy the boat, but that isn't going to be allowed to matter. At the dedication, Tracy Walker put away any resentment of those who hadn't come across; she was there for anybody who needed her.

"Chile, I wish you were here," said Mrs. Carter, and the word that kept coming up in her proud account of the day was "community"—the community did it. The morning offering—for the boat—was $1,151; the whole of the funds raised were gathered over the preceding year and a half and matched by the Reynoldses' Sapelo Island Research Foundation. Another speaker at the service celebrating the community for looking out for itself this way was one of Sapelo's people come home.

"I'm born and bred Sapelo," begins Charles Hall when I reach him on the telephone to ask him how the dedication went. I've tracked him in Dayton, Ohio, and immediately we're into a rich island conversation. When Hall was a little boy—he was born in 1934—his Walker grandmother still lived at Raccoon Bluff. From her place he climbed down the twelve-foot banks to fish in Blackbeard Creek.

That fishing (which he comes back to from Ohio whenever he can get away) became a summertime and holiday thing when Charles graduated from the island's grammar school. His parents put stock in education, and he and later his brother Benjamin were sent to live with an aunt on the mainland for high school.

Then begins the classic American success story; Charles (and Benjamin too) went on to Morehouse College in Atlanta. I asked Mr. Hall if he felt like a country boy in the big city attending a college that takes its social status exceedingly seriously. No, he said; he'd struggled with and mastered that feeling when he left the island for school in the coastal almost-city of Brunswick forty miles—and light-years—away. He got over being intimidated before he got to Atlanta.

Charles Hall was at Morehouse in its greatest days. He was there after Martin Luther King, Jr.'s, time, but in classes with him were Maynard Jackson, recently Atlanta's mayor, and Louis Sullivan, the former secretary of human services. More to the point was the presence of Benjamin Mays. The tall, imposing president of the college was a persuasive force a student failed to reckon with at his peril. At compulsory chapel after chapel, Mays made Hall and his fellows feel they had no option other than to excel. There were changes in the world that needed making. They wouldn't be made unless black men were twice as able as the white ones blocking them.

The rehabilitations that Charles Hall achieved were physical rather than political. After Morehouse, he took a graduate degree in physical therapy at the University of Pittsburgh and practiced first at the Veterans Hospital in Tuskegee, Alabama, and then, as an officer in the United States Air Force, at the Wright-Patterson Air Force Base in Dayton. He is president of a physical therapy corporation in that city now and head too of a home health agency which reaches into hospitals and nursing homes as well as promoting preventive treatment in public schools and homes.

Home is in Ohio now, but it is to his first home that he has come back to celebrate *Miss St. Luke* on August 23, 1992. But there is nothing down-home about the way Hall describes the community; he uses the anthropological term "fictive family." He knew perfectly well that he was related to half the people listening to him in St. Luke's, and insists that what matters is not the relationship by blood—interestingly, his children are adopted—or by marriage, but some other cement of common place and purpose.

Success is an Atlanta word that doesn't make much sense on Sapelo. But Charles Hall used it at St. Luke's, and what the word meant was the boat that was not an individual's but was theirs. That successful link to the world—and back from it to a place more valuable—could not have been achieved if someone had said "You can't do it" to Tracy Walker, and Walker had listened. The determination to do something, to get the boat, drew not at all on a competitive desire to push one individual ahead of another. As Hall expressed it, it came from the book— from Paul to the Corinthians:

> Finally, brothers and sisters, farewell. Be perfect, be of good comfort, be of one mind, live in peace; and the God of love and peace shall be with you.

I have taken much from my exploration of Sapelo, and with the taking comes the urge to give back. But all I have to offer is these stories, and as I look over them I am aware of how much is not here. I have not met every person in Hog Hammock, not traced its twentieth-century political economy. I have not written biographies of Matty Carter, Allen Green, or Glasco Bailey, have only sketched the career of Elizabeth Elaine Lemon and Charles Hall, and predicted (with fingers crossed) a future for Shannon and James Banks, Jr. Have I sold them all short?

On reflection, I don't think so. In Norman Maclean's brilliant telling of that terrible August 5, 1949, when thirteen young men died in the horror of a forest fire gone wild, he, with almost agonizing passion, gave those men back their day, by re-creating each desperately gained yard and each minute of the close of their lives. But he felt no need to tell us much of anything of their lives prior to that day.

I do not think I need to force Mrs. Carter, or Mr. Green, or Mr. Bailey back through the eight decades of their lives. That would not be a gift. That past, in all its pride, its pain, its down-to-earth ordinariness, its glory, seen from the present is theirs alone. I know because my own past is as dented and as fine as theirs and, in the whole scheme of things, not very different—or less long.

No, what I would like to give to Sapelo's people is what Robert Penn Warren so magnificently recognized was about the best gift in our power to give—the past from which we, all of us, came. One of my students, working within the grim constraints of a dissertation, discovered in another Georgia county a man named Abram Colby, who fought with such valiance for the rights of his people during Reconstruction, was so capable in his political activities, that he was brutally beaten and probably killed (there is no record of his ending). What troubled Jonathan Bryant was that when he talked at length with a good many descendants of the people with whom Colby had worked, not one of them had heard of the man.

Sapelo seems too gentle for a Colby, though it had its Toby Maxwell. Twenty-year-olds don't often talk of peacefulness, but that's the word James Banks uses when he talks about coming home. And there is beauty. On a winter's cold, clear morning, with almost-frosted foam from a rough sea shilly-shallying along the flat gray sand, Sapelo's dune-backed beach is a wonder of the world. Against its almost monochromatic whites and grays stand the rich bronze and chestnut of the islanders themselves. There is handsomeness rather than heroics.

There has been sadness, of course. Driving down to go out to the island most recently, I took the turn at the shrimpers' dock and I could see the top of the wheelhouse of the *Sapelo Queen* standing at her wharf. Crossing the bridge over the tag end of inlet and turning left on the narrow road up to the dock I found myself driving through a sea of people disembarking. The three-o'clock boat had come into Meridian from Sapelo. I learned later that it was a second run; three hundred people had gone over to the island for the funeral.

Now they were coming back—in suits, hats, and ties, in bold black-and-white dresses and black patent-leather shoes. There was something Irish about it all; if not a wake, there had been its Southern American equivalent—hours of public church and graveyard grief, now expelled. (Personal pain had already found its time and would again.) Subdued, people were amiably chatting and parting. A parade of Glynn and McIntosh County license plates signaled their swift going, which left the dock empty of all except the captain, Tracy Walker, and his two crewmen.

Senseless was the word that entered every conversation about Kendall Banks's death. It was two young men fighting over a girl. In the old days, everybody agreed, two strong (and lusty) young men would have hauled off and gone after each other with their fists. There would have been bloody and broken noses and the fight would have had an ending—and, perhaps, the field sown for a much-later reconciliation. But in 1992 in Brunswick, Georgia—in America—the two men had guns, fired and killed each other.

A friend had told me about the funeral when I called to borrow his characteristically battered Sapelo Chevrolet Suburban, whose not-great age was already lost in island vehicular immortality. It would be being used to carry people to the service; I was to pick it up at Marsh Landing when that duty was done. Standing on the top deck on the way out to the island later that afternoon—the five-fifteen trip was almost empty—I got talking to a young man who had been at the funeral. (He had taken the earlier boat to do an errand on the mainland and was on his way back to stay with his grandmother.)

The man they buried had been a high school friend, but he wasn't satisfied with how the service had gone; he wanted a band, a New Orleans band, at his funeral—it would be a party. (I didn't ask if he realized that those bands play dirges.) Birth is when you should mourn, he said. In a philosophical discourse on life and death there is not apt to be much said that is new, not much that can startle, and, quickly, I got his point. "You come into a life of sin; when you leave you go to glory."

This response to the day's burial hadn't occurred to me. But it did make me glad that I had not gone to the funeral; senseless still seemed more like the right word to me. Attending a Sapelo funeral—to complete my course that had included an anniversary celebration, the ordination of a deacon, and a couple of regular three-hour Sunday-morning services—would have been an intensely interesting experience. But I was glad I had skipped class.

I'm not a sociologist and not a reporter. I do have a personal connection now to some of the communicants of the First ABC. But not enough, I thought, to the man being buried to justify my walking into the church that day. In fact, it was only in a long quiet talk with James Banks, Jr., the next evening that I realized who he was. The man they buried was James's first cousin, Kendall Banks, the energetic, lithe man to whom, a year and a half earlier, in warm May sunlight after the anniversary service, I had introduced myself.

And for whom I had imagined a bright future. Enviously, I had thought that anyone with a body like that deserved the world. Had I gone to the funeral, I would have seen that body a corpse. I preferred the distant memory, but early the next morning, a Sunday, not twenty-four hours after they put him in the ground, I went alone to Behavior.

I passed three 1992 interments before coming on the fresh earth of Kendall's grave. Piled on the mound of loam was the usual crowding of plastic floral wreaths perched on wire stakes. (They won't decompose; they make a sad tiny trash heap of the graves as the months go by.) But someone had brought fall chrysanthemums cut from a garden, and, better still, others had heeled some living plants into the forest-rich loam of Behavior. The bird-of-paradise won't make it, but maybe the two azaleas will.

This is the first time that Behavior has smacked of the present for me. Soon grass will climb over the mound of dirt arching over his coffin. Soon Kendall Banks will recede into the history of an island that has seemed to endure too much of the past. But, precisely because of that weight, Sapelo's people deserve to have their past back.

I will have discharged a small part of my debt to the

island if I can tell a bit of its story. (Debt, not guilt; no word has done less useful service to the relations between those in America who have been forced to categorize ourselves as black and white.) I want to give back to Sapelo's people Sapelo's people: the slavery people, the Civil War people, the Reconstruction people, those who once lived in all of the island's hammocks. That's what I must do when I leave.

I'm standing alone on the Post Office Landing dock. In old Charles Hall's day, the mail came in here; it doesn't anymore. Like almost everything and everybody, except the poaching forays of the realtors onto the island's north end, the mail comes in through the state's Marsh Landing. It's just as well that the state maintains that control; none would be disastrous. And that focus leaves the Post Office Landing dock wonderfully alone. Standing on its planks and leaning on the tops of pilings high out of a middle tide in a quiet dusk, I'm haunted by the triumphant loneliness and uneasy serenity of the island.

My back is not to a second-growth forest, but probably a tenth-; the island is so much older than its trees, though the great oaks of Hog Hammock try to tell me otherwise. And farther behind me lies the rich texture of the salt marsh and then the majestic beach, flat, plain, and commanding. Now all that is below me is the water, dirty and lazily swirling. Ugly mussels cling by beards to the tide line of the pilings. Before me is nothing but a maze of islands made of no clay save that which holds up the relentless vertical spartina grass.

Miss St. Luke is tied up at this dock—its coming and

going will not be at the state's pleasure—but I am not to be her passenger. Instead, I'm waiting for a ride I've arranged for, and as I wait—fighting off impatience—I almost plead with myself to bring back that sunset over Doboy Sound that on an earlier waiting had been so beautiful. But the picture won't come, won't because it is time for me to go. I'll come back to Sapelo and time and time again I'll try to understand Hog Hammock, to know its people. They arrest me more strongly than almost any others in a long life of being held fast to curiosity about people. On each trip, I'll gain a little more knowledge of the island, talk more with its people.

But there will be losses too. Even as new things are put in place, other things will slip away. A house will go up to mar the marsh; another Carter or Green will die.[*] And so Behavior will be added to. Its hold on the future, on the earth, will have increased. And, in candor, we must know that, each day, our hold on Hog Hammock's past is decreased by a relentless present. Subtracted from, but not lost, because Sapelo's burial ground behaves as it wants to. It depends on no great, inscribed gates to proclaim its significance, no neatly trimmed alleys to order the cluster of families.

There is just the whiff of the comic in Behavior as there is all through Hog Hammock. Somehow, all the people back to Bilali, if not to the Indians lost to the island decades before he was forced to found it, endured in part

---

[*] Or Bailey. Even as this reaches the printer, Greg Bailey, Cornelia and Julius's young son, murdered in Brunswick, was brought home and, in a fall rain, laid to rest in Behavior. His friends and the island's elders, together, lowered shovel after shovel of Sapelo onto his coffin. And planted flowers.

because something wildly funny propped open the flap of a sad tent and let the light in. We all whistle past the graveyard. But Behavior whistles back. Way off on the Post Office Landing dock I can almost hear a reminder that Minto Bell lies there. And, somehow, something of me does too. I'm implicated. Impatient as I now am to be away, I know that Behavior, that all of her people, will be whispering at my shoulder long after I've climbed into the motorboat—almost out of gas—crazily, confidently maneuvered by the white wife of a white fisherman coming for me from Valona.

Waiting, the maze of grass clumps seems so endlessly bewildering that I'm not even sure which way the meandering channel runs to water open to the mainland. Not even the clear call of a bird matters; nothing makes sense. I want to get away, not so much to escape as to get back so that I can try to make sense of where I've been. Far off—at last—there is the sound of a boat's small motor. The woman at the wheel will find her way to the dock—to take me back. But even then, I'm not sure the island will let me go. Not sure I want it to.

AFTERWORD

There are many things that this book is not. It is not a history of Sapelo, and it is not a position paper addressing the problems those living on the island face in relation to those powerful enough to compound or alleviate those problems. And I have not attempted monographs on slavery, war refugees, or Reconstruction. The archival work that I have done has only scratched the topsoil of the vast sources that exist; far more, for example, on the freed people of Sapelo's resistance to their removal from the lands they had begun tending in 1865 could be done. A full account of Reconstruction on the Georgia sea islands similar to Willie Lee Rose's study of the South Carolina islands would be excellent to have.

What the book is, if this is not to use too grand a varnish, is a meditation on race. After thirty years of scholarly cogitation and more than fifty of head scratching, I still don't quite know what race is. But it is. All of my work has confronted that fact—studies of the Freedmen's

Bureau, of a Civil War general and Reconstruction president, and of one of the most interesting nineteenth-century Americans, one who winced at being incessantly referred to as a leader of his race. (I am not sure that even Frederick Douglass, who certainly knew, as few of us do, who he was, knew with any certainty what the word signified.)

As I focused on Oliver Otis Howard, Ulysses S. Grant, and Douglass, I tried to look past them to less celebrated Americans who, it has always seemed to me, knew who they were, but who perplexed their more powerful neighbors. It was not so much that I wanted to understand how that puzzlement turned into hateful actions, as it was that I needed to try, at least, to know the slaves and freed people—and their descendants—with whom I share an American history.

Sapelo's people, with their sensibly cautious welcome, gave me a direct chance to get acquainted with those I previously had been able to glimpse only past the shoulders of Great Men. To achieve that acquaintance, I recalled what a good many students have taught me over the years. Both in the classroom and on the island, it has seemed to me that, for better or worse, I had better be myself. I hope that that honesty, betraying not too much naivete, has resulted in a convincing portrayal of some people of whom I have become exceedingly fond.

I was struck as I worked on this book with the sharp contrast between my story and the one told so well by Melissa Fay Greene in *Praying for Sheetrock*, which is set in the same, small McIntosh County. Her book is vastly different from mine not only because hers is a story of political events, locally and beautifully focused, but because life along Route 17, just inland from Meridian and running north to south through Darien—once the main route from New York to Florida—was distinct from that lived only a few miles away by people, some of them relatives, out on Sapelo. To a degree, at least, islands are unto themselves.

I have received a large amount of help in the writing of this small book. My greatest debt is to Mae Ruth Green, who traced forty-four Sapelo families over close to two centuries. I know of no other study of a group of American families that is comparable. Hers is a labor of love. performed with great skill. Those who think there is no value in hewing to formal discipline when writing history could usefully compare her tightly delineated genealogies with the sentimental "gleanings" of would-be affectionate observers. On the other hand, those who think the heart should be left in the cloakroom when entering history's classroom should (but won't) be instructed by the extent to which she permitted her respect for the people she was studying to shine through her work.

I drew heavily on Russell Duncan's *Freedom's Shore* and on our rich friendship. Another good friend, Kim Townsend, worked through a philosophical point with me. Michael Gibson, and, particularly, Keith Bohannon (an accomplished sleuth), graduate students at the University of Georgia, helped greatly with research. Another, Lori Cline, proved to be an editor with a keen, sensitive eye. Solving the mysteries of the Bilali manuscript was fascinating and I am deeply grateful to University of Georgia librarians, Mary Ellen Brooks, the late Larry Gulley, and William Potter for arranging for the dating of the document. Sara Lochmiller's painstaking photographs of the manuscript enabled me to consult people not in Athens as to its contents. Bradford Martin, who has an article forthcoming on the subject, labored long to translate as much as can be read of Bilali's work, and Ahmad Dallal gave the sensitive reading that I discussed in the text.

On Sapelo, Cornelia Bailey generously shared her unparalleled command of the island's history. She is at work writing that history "from the inside," and it will be wonderful to have her book. In addition, as the text attests, I am indebted more than I can say for all the friendly and informative conversations with other residents of Hog Hammock. Let me add just one last time how much visits with Matty Carter, Glasco Bailey, and Allen Green meant to me. And I value greatly the friendly, informative conversations I had with James Banks, Jr.

Lorene Townsend, librarian of the University of Georgia's Marine Institute on Sapelo, generously shared the materials she has collected on her neighbors. Buddy Sullivan, historian of McIntosh County and now engaged in interpretation of the island's history for visitors, went out of his way to get answers to questions and his *Early Days in Tidewater Georgia* contains information that I found indispensable. Jody Sasser of the *Darien News* confirmed facts and the reference librarians at the Georgia Historical Society archives in Savannah provided crucial information.

I had many conversations with friends of the island as I made my way into this book. Kenneth Thomas alerted me to Mae Ruth Green's work, and Reita Rivers generously shared both tapes of oral interviews in her possession and her own knowledge of the community.

I owe great thanks to my good friends Milner and June

Ball who first took me to the island, and to other friends who kept me going—including Stephen Lucas, John Inscoe, Bertis and Katherine Downs, Philip Hamburger, Jack Leigh, Maureen McGarty, Andy Miller, and Barry Werth. My colleague David Schoenbrun was most helpful on African matters and Jacqueline Jones went out of her way to assist with my discussion of Sapelo's schools. On the island, Caesar and Nancy Banks were wonderful hosts.

I am deeply grateful not only to my teaching colleagues at the University of Georgia, but also to the officials of the university for the fine support that I have had for my writing. The Richard B. Russell Foundation generously supplied funds for travel and research. Thanks are due too to the good people at the W.E.B. Du Bois Institute at Harvard University, which has been my home away from home as I have worked on this book.

Two skillful readers, Drake McFeely and Mary Drake McFeely, gave helpful critiques of earlier drafts and Edward Johnson copy-edited the manuscript with care. Finally, once again, my deep gratitude to the whole of the Norton family.

W.S.M.
October 1993

Notes

Chapter 1: Meridian Dock

1. Georgia Department of Natural Resources and U.S. Department of Commerce, "Sapelo Island National Estuarine Research Reserve Management Plan" ([no place,] 1990), 8.

2. On October 23, 1993 (as this book was in press), Gregory Pernell Bailey, twenty-five, "Sapelo Island native" and graduate of McIntosh County Academy, Class of '86, died at Southeast Georgia Regional Medical Center in Brunswick. His funeral, on October 30, was in St. Luke's Church. *Darien News*, Nov. 4, 1993, and Josephine Beoku-Betts to the author. (See p. 169.)

3. The state is in the process of shifting jurisdiction over the house from the university to the Department of Natural Resources.

Chapter 2: Hog Hammock

1. Quotations from conversations, recorded in my notes, will not be annotated. Genealogical information is from Mae

Ruth Green, "Sapelo Island Families," studies of forty-four families, Department of Natural Resources, Real Estate Division, Atlanta, Georgia.

2. Green, op. cit., "March Carter," Family #106, lists eight siblings; perhaps two were not reported to her; perhaps Matty Carter's memory was in error. In this case, I have followed her recollection. Memory, with all of its tricky fallibility and its rich veracity, is one of the things that this book is about.

Chapter 3: Behavior

1. In 1857, Bilali was said to have "died recently." W. B. Hodgson, "The Gospels: Written in the Negro Patois of English, with Arabic Characters," paper read at Ethnological Society of New York, October 13, 1857, typescript, Hargrett Room, University of Georgia Library. In 1931, the son of Francis R. Goulding stated that Bilali gave the document to Goulding, a minister and historian, when the slave was "old and crippled and not able to work . . . [and] lived on the mainland just opposite Sapelo Island where my father visited him often and had numerous interviews with him." "Affidavit of Capt. Benjamin Lloyd Goulding as to Arabic Document," October 12, 1931, typescript, Hargrett Room, where the Bilali document itself is now housed.

2. Roderick McNeil, "Auger Microscopy Analysis of Penetration of Iron Fibers into the Document's Paper," September 1993, Hargrett Room, University of Georgia Library.

3. Joseph H. Greenberg, "The Decipherment of the 'Ben-Ali Diary,' " *Journal of Negro History*, vol. 25, no. 3 (July 1940): 372–75.

4. Ulrich B. Phillips, *American Negro Slavery* (Baton Rouge: Louisiana State University Press, 1966), 94.

5. Philip Curtin, *The Atlantic Slave Trade: A Census* (Madison: University of Wisconsin Press, 1969), 140.

6. Philip Curtin, "Jihad in West Africa: Early Phases and Inter-relations in Mauretania and Senegal," *Journal of American History* 12 (1971), 11–24, quoted in Peter B. Clarke, *West Africa and Islam: A Study of Religious Development from the 18th to the 20th Centuries* (London: E. Arnold, 1982), 84.

7. Translation of Bradford J. Martin, article in *Georgia Historical Quarterly*, forthcoming.

8. William B. Hodgeson, *Notes on Northern Africa, the Sahara and Soudan* (New York: Wiley and Putnam, 1844), 74.

9. There have been several attempts at translation of the document. Bradford J. Martin, a scholar of West African religion, reconstructed much of it; the rendering of the instructions for ritual washing is his. Ahmad Dallal, a thoughtful scholar of the culture of the region, has gotten closer to Bilali's work than any previous investigator with his intelligent conjecture as to how the document was created. I am particularly grateful for his help.

10. Dallal's rendering.

11. E. Merton Coulter, *Thomas Spalding of Sapelo* (Baton Rouge: Louisiana State University Press, 1940).

12. A claim is made that early in the eighteenth century, coastal planters may have developed a strain of long-staple cotton on their own and did not need to import the seed from the Bahamas. But the vast increase in the quantity raised (9,840 pounds were exported from Charleston in 1789–90, 8,301,907 pounds in 1800–1) argues that a great deal of seed (if not all of it) and laborers to clear the salt marshes so conducive to the raising of the cotton were imported from the Bahamas, where cultivation was well established. Charles F. Kovacik and Robert E. Mason, "Changes in the South Carolina Sea Island Cotton Industry," *Southeast Geographer* 25,2 (Nov. 1985), 77–104, 79, 83.

13. One planter complained of a balky early long-staple gin: "My negroes continually putting it out of order, and my impelling

power proving defective, I laid it aside. I introduce this remark, hoping that the want of a gin, as well adapted to the Sea-Island cotton as Whitney's saw gin is to the upland, may stimulate some of our planters . . . to produce one." "A Mr. McCarthy" of Florida did so in 1840. Thomas Aston Coffin to Whitemarsh B. Seabrook, Dec. 26, 1826, in W. B. Seabrook, A *Report Accompanied by Sundry Letters on the Causes Which Contribute to the Production of Fine Sea-Island Cotton* (Charleston: A. E. Miller, 1827); Lewis C. Gray, *History of Agriculture in the Southern United States to 1860* (Gloucester, Mass.: Peter Smith, 1958), 2: 736.

14. Charles Spalding Wylly, "The Story of Sapeloe," typescript, 1915, Library of Marine Institute, Sapelo Island, Ga., 19. Slave importations were illegal in South Carolina from 1787 to 1803; the reopening of an import market was authorized by the legislature in 1803; it was closed under the constitutional prohibition in 1808. Walter J. Fraser, Jr., *Charleston! Charleston! The History of a Southern City* (Columbia: University of South Carolina Press, 1989), 188.

15. Savannah Unit, Georgia Writers' Project, Work Projects Administration, *Drums and Shadows: Survival Studies Among the Georgia Coastal Negroes* (Athens: University of Georgia Press, 1986) [reprint of 1940 edition], 161.

16. Georgia Bryan Conrad, "Reminiscences of a Southern Woman," *Southern Workman*, vol. 30, no. 5 (May 1901): unpaged.

17. W. B. Swaney to G. M. Shelby, Oct. 21, 1931, typescript, Hargrett Room, University of Georgia Library.

18. Conrad, "Reminiscenses," 19.

19. *Drums and Shadows*, 161.

20. Ibid., 162.

21. Ibid., 161.

22. "Gullah: A Creole Language," chapter 7 of Charles Joyner, *Down by the Riverside: A South Carolina Slave Community* (Urbana: University of Illinois Press, 1984), 196–224. The

makers of the language were slaves, many Muslim, and many who learned English in the West Indies before coming to Georgia. This collective language was important to later slaves coming directly from Africa.

23. *Drums and Shadows*, 162.
24. Ibid.
25. Ibid.
26. Coulter, *Thomas Spalding*, 90–91.

Chapter 4: "A Wild African Tribe"

1. *Drums and Shadows*, 163. The census taker in 1870 recorded "Guinea" as the place of birth of both Carolina and Hannah Underwood. This could be accurate, or it could be an example of the frequent use of "Guinea" as a name for anywhere in Africa that African Americans came from. There are other explicit statements that the Underwoods were Ibo.
2. It is likely that the "peanuts" were bambara ground nuts.
3. *Drums and Shadows*, 163.
4. Ellen Barrow Spalding to Charles Wylly, August 1914, in Robert L. Humphries, ed., *The Journal of Archibald C. McKinley* (Athens: University of Georgia Press, 1991), 242.
5. Wylly, "Story of Sapeloe," 31.
6. Ibid., 31.
7. Ibid., 37.
8. Ibid., 39.
9. Ibid.
10. Ibid.
11. Ibid.
12. Ibid., 42.
13. Ibid., 40.
14. Wylly quoting H. E. Coffin's record of a conversation the two held in December 1913, ibid., 146.
15. Ibid., 39, 41.

16. Ibid., 41.
17. Coulter, *Thomas Spalding*, 82.
18. Wylly, "Story of Sapeloe," 42.
19. Ibid., 23.
20. John Mackintosh Moore, *et al.*, to James Oglethorpe, January 3, 1738–9, in Allen D. Candler, comp., *Colonial Records of Georgia* (Atlanta: Franklin Printing and Publishing, 1905), 3: 427–28.
21. Wylly, "Story of Sapeloe," 23.
22. Ibid., 42.

Chapter 5: Marsh Landing

1. Coulter, *Thomas Spalding*, 82.
2. There was, in the eighteenth century near Fernandina, Florida, an interesting interracial maroon colony composed partially of runaway Georgia slaves.
3. Quoted on catalogue card, Charles Spalding to Adjutant General Wayne, February 11, 1861, Georgia Department of Archives and History; actual letter unlocated.
4. Charles C. Jones, Jr., to the "Rev. and Mrs. C. C. Jones," Nov. 9, 1861, in Robert Manson Myers, *Children of Pride: A True Story of Georgia and the Civil War* (New Haven, Conn.: Yale University Press, 1972), 792.
5. When Thomas Spalding died in 1851, he bypassed his two living sons to leave the bulk of his Sapelo holdings to his grandson, Thomas Spalding, who reached his majority, twenty-one, only in 1868. This second Thomas Spalding was the son of Randolph Spalding; Randolph and his sister Catherine Spalding Kenan were the only members of that generation to continue to live on Sapelo. Catherine was also left considerable acreage and many slaves. After his father's death, Randolph lived in the big house with his wife, Mary

Bass Spalding; his daughter, Sarah; and his two sons, Thomas and Thomas Bourke. After Randolph's death in 1862, Thomas's uncle Charles Spalding, who lived on the mainland, was the executor of his brother's will, but Mary Bass Spalding was the active head of her branch of the family.

6. Buddy Sullivan, *Early Days on the Georgia Tidewater: The Story of McIntosh County and Sapelo* (Darien, Ga.: McIntosh County Board of Commissioners, 1990), 787.

7. Ella Barrow Spalding to Charles Spalding Wylly, August 1914, in Humphries, *Journal of McKinley*, 239.

8. Ophelia Wilson Holmes orally to Mae Ruth Green, in Green, op. cit., "Boson Gardner Family," Family #109.

9. Russell Duncan, introduction to Humphries, *Journal of McKinley*, xxxiv; interview by Fred McMurray with Charles Hall, in unpaged appendix to Jana Earl Hesser, "Historical, Demographic, and Biochemical Studies on Sapelo Island," M.A. thesis, University of Pennsylvania, [1970].

10. McMurray interview.

11. Green, op. cit., "John Brown Family," Family #104, quoting Katie Brown in Lydia Parrish, *Slave Songs of the Georgia Sea Islands* (Hatboro, Pa.: Folklore Association, 1965), 131.

12. Samuel Pellman Boyer, Diary, Feb. 21, 1863, quoted in Sullivan, *Early Days*, 310.

13. Thomas Wentworth Higginson, *Army Life in a Black Regiment* (New York: Norton, 1984), 40.

14. Ibid., 40n.

15. Ibid., 45.

16. Ibid., 48.

17. Ibid., 153.

18. Ibid., 154.

19. Ibid., 155.

20. Ibid., 158–59, 161.

21. Federal Government Pension Records #897-641, March

Wilson, quoted in Green, op. cit., "March Wilson Family," Family #142.

22. Service Record, March Wilson, Co. B., 33 USCT, National Archives.

23. Allen Green is a deacon (and pillar) of the African First Baptist Church, but he was on the deacon's bench in St. Luke's on December 8, 1991.

24. Allen Green's vague memories of mention by his grandfather of Macon, of Alabama, leave open the possibility that Allen Smith, born "c. 1835," might have been "adopted" into the Smith family during or immediately after the Civil War. Such extensions of families were common in the turbulence of the times. The physical description of Allen Smith—he was small—suggests this possibility. On the other hand, at thirty, the resourceful man would have been too old to need taking in; he is firmly recorded as the son of "Belali Smith" in both Allen Green's memory and Green, op. cit., "Hester Smith Family," Family #134.

25. Boyer Diary, June 11, 1863, in Sullivan, *Early Days*, 312–13.

26. Ibid., 312.

27. Ibid.

28. Ibid., 313.

29. Dr. James Holmes (who remained in McIntosh County throughout the war) published reminiscences in the *Darien Timber Gazette*, April 14 and 21, 1876, quoted in Sullivan, *Early Days*, 324.

30. Ella Barrow Spalding to Charles Spalding Wylly, August 1914, quoted in Humphries, *Journal of McKinley*, 239.

31. United States Army pension records for James Lemon #598791 and Jane Lemon #447205, quoted in Green, op. cit., "James Lemon Family," Family #121.

32. Mae Ruth Green interview with Elizabeth Elaine Lemon, Eulonia, Georgia, January 1983, "James Lemon Family," Family #121.

33. Cornelius V. Troup, *Distinguished Negro Georgians* (Dallas: Royal Publishing, 1962), 105; *Who's Who of American Women: 1977–1978* (Chicago: Marquis, 1978), 525.

Chapter 6: Coming Home

1. Resa Smith and her son Gibb, Charles Hall to Fred McMurray, Appendix 1 of Hesser, "Studies on Sapelo Island," unpaged.
2. Shelby Foote, *The Civil War: A Narrative*, 3 vols. (New York: Random House, 1958–74), 3: 640–41.
3. William Tecumseh Sherman, quoted in ibid., 3: 644.
4. Ibid., 645.
5. Ibid., 649.
6. Burke Davis, *Sherman's March* (New York: Random House, 1980), 91.
7. Ibid., 92.
8. Foote, *Civil War*, 3: 649.
9. Burke, *Sherman's March*, 93.
10. Ibid.
11. Russell Duncan, *Freedom's Shore: Tunis Campbell and the Georgia Freedmen* (Athens: University of Georgia Press, 1986), 18.
12. Ibid., 19.
13. William Tecumseh Sherman, *Memoirs of General W. T. Sherman* (New York: Library of America, 1990), 730.
14. Ibid.
15. National Archives, Record Group 105, Bureau of Refugees Freedmen and Abandoned Lands, microfilm, Harvard University Library, microfilm 798, reel 36, 38, 56. I have been unable to ascertain with certainty which, if any, of the five possible male Wilsons among the Spaldings' former slaves Fergus Wilson was. Fuller Wilson is the most likely candidate. Mae Ruth Green, "Benjamin Wilson," Family #141.
16. On June 9, 1841, Thomas Spalding "in consideration of the

love and affection for my daughter Catherine and the future benefit of my grand children and in consideration of one cent in hand paid" by her husband and brother, anticipated his will of 1835 and presented Catherine Spalding Kenan with sixty slaves whose first names only are appended. McIntosh County, Ga., deed book B, pp. 208–11, microfilm, Georgia Department of Archives and History, Atlanta. Sullivan, *Early Times*, 787, lists 199 slaves belonging to Michael J. Kenan in 1850.

17. Green, op. cit., "John Brown Family," Family #104, quoting Parrish, *Slave Songs*, 131.

18. National Archives, RG 105, M798, reel 36, p. 152.

19. Charles H. Howard, report to the Freedmen's Bureau, cited in Duncan, *Freedom's Shore*, 33.

20. "Laws of the United States," *Congressional Globe*, 38th Cong., 2nd sess., 1865, Appendix, 141.

21. Robert Frost, "The Gift Outright," in *Collected Poems of Robert Frost* (Garden City, N.Y.: Henry Holt, 1942), 745.

22. Sherman, *Memoirs*, 731.

23. Duncan, *Freedom's Shore*, 16.

24. Ibid., 22.

Chapter 7: Hanging Bull

1. *New York Tribune*, March 9, 1859. Clipping in the possession of Lorene Townsend, Darien, Ga. For a fine account of this grim business, see Malcolm Bell, Jr., *Major Butler's Legacy: Five Generations of a Slaveholding Family* (Athens: University of Georgia Press, 1987), 327–40.

2. Coulter, *Thomas Spalding*, 85.

3. Duncan, *Freedom's Shore*, 25.

4. Anthony Wilson to E. P. Smith, Sept. 30, 1870. Teaching in Woodbine in 1870, Wilson named a second school Sun Shine; Anthony Wilson (on formal reporting form) to American Missionary Association, January 1870, photocopy from

American Missionary Archive, Fisk University, Nashville. Wilson does not appear on the 1870 census for Sapelo; that tallying was done in the summer of 1869—he may have been a new teacher that fall.

5. 1870 Manuscript Census, Sapelo Island, McIntosh County, microfilm, University of Georgia Library.

6. Ibid.

7. Charley Lemon *et al.* to American Missionary Association, March 28, 1870, American Missionary Association Archive, Fisk University, microfilm, University of Georgia Library.

8. "Sun Shine School," Sapelo Island, to "Messrs," American Missionary Association, May 10, 1870, AMA, microfilm.

9. Charles Marshall, Sapelo Island, to Edward P. Smith, American Missionary Association, April 1, 18, May 1, 1870, AMA, microfilm.

10. Simms North, Atlanta, to E. P. Smith, American Missionary Association, August 20, 1870, AMA, microfilm.

11. Ibid.

12. Charles H. Joiner, ed., *A History of Public Education in Georgia, 1734–1976* (Columbia, S.C.: R. L. Bryan, 1979), 73.

13. Ibid.

14. Ibid., 72.

15. Ibid., 75.

16. Jacqueline Jones, *Soldiers of Light and Love: Northern Teachers and Georgia Blacks, 1865–1873* (Athens: University of Georgia Press, 1992).

17. S. P. Harrold to E. P. Smith, April 12, 1869, quoted in Duncan, *Freedom's Shore*, 63.

Chapter 8: First African Baptist Church

1. Ella Barrow Spalding to Charles Spalding Wylly, August 1914, Humphries, *Journal of McKinley*, 242.

2. Green, op. cit., "Prince Carter Family," Family #107.

3. Duncan, *Freedom's Shore*, 43–44.

4. Ibid., 45.

5. Green, op. cit., "Charles Jones Family," Family #119; Sullivan, *Early Days*, 338, 473; Buddy Sullivan telephone call to the author, reporting conversation with Charles Jones, August 11, 1993.

Chapter 9: Raccoon Bluff

1. William Tecumseh Sherman, Special Field Orders No. 15, Jan. 16, 1865, in Sherman, *Memoirs*, 730.

2. Ellen Barrow Spalding to Charles Spalding Wylly, August 1914, in Humphries, *Journal of McKinley*, 239.

3. William Faulkner, *The Unvanquished* (New York: Vintage, 1966), 216.

4. National Archives, RG 105, M798, reel 36, pp. 22, 27. Thomas Mills settled twenty-five acres; Hercules Bennett fifteen; there appears to have been only one forty-acre unit. Paul A. Cimbala, "The Terms of Freedom: The Freedmen's Bureau and Reconstruction in Georgia, 1865–1870," Ph.D. diss., Emory University, 1983.

5. Ibid., p. 96.

6. Ibid., 166, 6.

7. "Laws of the United States," 141.

8. William S. McFeely, *Yankee Stepfather: General O. O. Howard and the Freedmen* (New York: Norton, 1970), 103.

9. O. O. Howard, BRFAL Circular 13, July 28, 1865, in ibid., 104.

10. Ibid., 121.

11. Ibid.

12. Ibid., 147.

13. Ibid., 127.

14. Toby Maxwell deposition (signed with his X) [May 20, 1872], submitted to Committee of the Georgia Senate

investigating charges against Tunis Campbell, Georgia Department of Archives and History, Atlanta.

15. Russell Duncan, introduction to Humphries, *Journal of McKinley*, xxvii.

16. Samuel Ross deposition, signed apparently in his own hand, [May 20, 1872], submitted to Committee of the Georgia Senate investigating Tunis Campbell, Georgia Department of Archives and History, Atlanta.

17. Ross deposition.

18. Duncan, *Freedom's Shore*, 34.

19. Ibid.

20. I do not have fully verifable evidence that the Maxwells were brothers, but their ages and the prominence of the Maxwell family on the island suggests that they were.

21. Ella Barrow Spalding to Charles Spalding Wylly, August 1914, in Humphries, *Journal of McKinley*, 241.

22. Ibid., 240.

23. Maxwell deposition.

24. Ella Barrow Spalding to Charles Spalding Wylly, in Humphries, *Journal of McKinley*, 240.

25. Maxwell deposition.

26. Ibid.; Edmund L. Drago, *Black Politicians and Reconstruction in Georgia: A Splendid Failure* (Baton Rouge: Louisiana State University Press, 1982), 82.

27. Duncan, introduction to Humphries, *Journal of McKinley*, xxviii.

28. Ella Barrow Spalding to Charles Spalding Wylly, in ibid., 239.

29. 1870 Manuscript Census, microfilm, University of Georgia Library.

30. 1870 census. The census taker used the spelling "Spaulding" in the case both of Mary, Thomas, and Bourke Spalding, "W[hite]," and of Abram and Andrew Spaulding, "M[ulatto]." The pilot's, ship's carpenter's, and lighthouse

keeper's household numbers in the ledger immediately precede those of the white Spalding families—who are listed roughly in the middle of his reports of household visits.

31. Ella Barrow Spalding to Charles Spalding Wylly, in Humphries, *Journal of McKinley*, 248; Sullivan, *Early Days*, 602.

32. 1870 Manuscript Agricultural Census, microfilm, University of Georgia Library.

33. *Savannah Morning News*, cotton quotations, Sept. 2, 1870, microfilm, University of Georgia Library.

34. McIntosh County, Ga., Mortgage Book A, 11–12, photocopy of typescript in possession of Mae Ruth Green, Atlanta.

35. Mae Ruth Green, typescript notes from various mortgage and deed book records, McIntosh County Courthouse.

36. 1880 Manuscript Census, 1880 Manuscript Agricultural Census, microfilm, University of Georgia Library.

Chapter 10: Barn Creek

1. Cornelia Bailey, "Proceedings of the Sapelo Island Seminar," pamphlet, January 6, 1993, Southern Center for Continuing Education, Georgia Southern University, Statesboro, Ga. (Savannah: Georgia Conservancy, 1993), p. 12.

2. Wylly, "Story of Sapeloe," 27.

3. Sullivan, *Early Days*, 212.

4. Wylly, "Story of Sapeloe," 30.

5. James Walker to Ella Barrow Spalding, Nov. 4 (?), 1898, Spalding Family Papers, Georgia Historical Society, Savannah; Green, op. cit., "June Walker Family," Family #140.

6. Annie May Walker died September 15, 1993, at age 103, and was buried in Behavior.

Index